IRISH MELODIES

AND

SACRED SONGS.

IRISH MELODIES

AND

SACRED SONGS.

BY

THOMAS MOORE

FROM THE LAST EDITION OF HIS COLLECTED WORKS

New York and Boston:
C. S. FRANCIS AND COMPANY.
1854.

5380

63843

PREFACE.

(Originally prefixed to the Melodies in the collected edition of Moore's Works.)

THE recollections connected in my mind with that early period of my life, when I first thought of interpreting in verse the touching language of my country's music, tempt me again to advert to those long past days; and even at the risk of being thought to indulge overmuch in what Colley Cibber calls "the great pleasure of writing about one's self all day," to notice briefly some of those impressions and influences under which the attempt to adapt words to our ancient Melodies was for some time meditated by me, and, at last, undertaken.

There can be no doubt that to the zeal and industry of Mr. Bunting his country is indebted for the preservation of her old national airs. During the prevalence of the Penal Code, the music of Ireland was made to share in the fate of its people. Both were alike shut out from the pale of civilized life; and seldom any where but in the huts of the proscribed race could the sweet voice of the songs of other days be heard. Even of that class, the itinerant harpers, among whom for a long period our ancient music had been kept alive, there remained but few to continue the precious tradition; and a great music-meeting held at Belfast in the year 1792, at which the two or three still remaining of the old race of wandering harpers assisted, exhibited the last public effort made by the lovers of Irish music to preserve to their country the only grace or ornament left to her, out of the wreck of all her liberties and hopes. Thus what the fierce legislature of the Pale had endeavored vainly thro' so many centuries to effect,—the utter extinction of Ireland's Minstrelsy,—the deadly pressure of the Penal Laws had nearly, at the close of the eighteenth century, accomplished; and, but for the zeal and intelligent research of Mr. Bunting, at that crisis, the greater part of our musical treasures would probably have been lost to the world. It was in the year 1796 that this gentleman published his first volume; and the national spirit and hope, then wakened in Ireland by the rapid spread of the democratic principle throughout Europe, could not but insure a most cordial reception for such a work;—flattering as it was to the fond dreams of Erin's early days, and containing in itself, indeed, remarkable testimony to the truth of her claims to an early date of civilization.

It was in the year 1797 that, through the medium of Mr. Bunting's book, I was first made acquainted with the beauties of our native music.

A young friend of our family, Edward Hudson, the nephew of an eminent dentist of that name, who played with much taste and feeling on the flute, and unluckily for himself, was but too deeply warmed with the patriotic ardour then kindling around him, was the first who made known to me this rich mine of our country's melodies:—a mine, from the working of which my humble labours as a poet have since derived their sole lustre and value. About the same period I formed an acquaintance, which soon grew into intimacy, with young Robert Emmet. He was my senior, I think, by one class, in the university; for when, in the first year of my course, I became a member of the Debating Society,—a sort of nursery to the authorised Historical Society—I found him in full reputation, not only for his learning and eloquence, but also for the blamelessness of his life, and the grave suavity of his manners.

Of the political tone of this minor school of oratory, which was held weekly at the rooms of different resident members, some notion may be formed from the nature of the questions proposed for discussion,—one of which, I recollect, was, "Whether an Aristocracy or a Democracy is most favourable to the advancement of science and literature?" while another, bearing even more pointedly on the relative position of the government and the people, at this crisis, was thus significantly propounded:—"Whether a soldier was bound, on all occasions, to obey the orders of his commanding officer?" On the former of these questions, the effect of Emmet's eloquence upon his young auditors was, I recollect, most striking. The prohibition against touching upon modern politics, which it was subsequently found necessary to enforce, had not yet been introduced; and Emmet, who took of course ardently the side of democracy in the debate, after a brief review of the republics of antiquity, showing how much they had all done for the advancement of science and the arts, proceeded lastly to the grand and perilous example, then passing before all eyes, the young Republic of France. Referring to the circumstance told of Cæsar, that, in swimmiug across the Rubicon, he contrived to carry with him his Commentaries and his sword, the young orator said, "Thus France wades through a sea of storm and blood; but while, in one hand, she wields the sword against her aggressors, with the other she upholds the glories of science and literature, unsullied by the ensanguined tide through which she struggles." In another of his remarkable speeches, I remember his saying, "When a people advancing rapidly in knowledge and power perceive at last how far their government is lagging behind them, what then, I ask, is to be done in such a case? What, but to pull the government *up* to the people?"

In a few months after, both Emmet and myself were admitted members of the greater and recognised institution, called the Historical Society; and, even here, the political feeling so rife abroad contrived to mix up its restless spirit with all our debates and proceedings; notwithstanding the constant watchfulness of the college authorities, as well as of a strong party within the Society itself, devoted adherents to the policy of the government, and taking invariably part with the Provost and Fellows in all their restrictive and inquisitorial measures. The most distinguished and eloquent of these supporters of power were a young man named Sargent, of whose fate in after days I know nothing, and Jebb, the late bishop of Limerick, who was then, as he continued to be through life, much respected for his private worth and learning.

Of the popular side, in the Society, the chief champion and ornament was Robert Emmet; and though every care was taken to exclude from the subjects of debate all questions verging towards the politics of the day, it was always easy enough, by a side-wind of digression or allusion, to bring Ireland and the prospects then opening upon her within the scope of the orator's view. So exciting and powerful, in this respect, were Emmet's speeches, and so little were even the most eloquent of the adverse party able to cope with his powers, that it was at length thought advisable, by the higher authorities, to send among us a man of more advanced standing, as well as belonging to a former race of renowned speakers, in that Society, in order that he might answer the speeches of Emmet, and endeavour to obviate the mischievous impression they were thought to produce. The name of this mature champion of the higher powers it is not necessary here to record; but the object of his mission among us was in some respect gained; as it was in replying to a long oration of his, one night, that Emmet, much to the mortification of us who gloried in him as our leader, became suddenly embarrassed in the middle of his speech, and, to use the parliamentary phrase, broke down. Whether from a momentary confusion in the thread of his argument, or possibly from diffidence in encountering an adversary so much his senior,—for Emmet was as modest as he was high-minded and brave,—he began, in the full career of his eloquence, to hesitate and repeat his words, and then, after an effort or two to recover himself, sate down.

It fell to my own lot to be engaged, about the same time, in a brisk struggle with the dominant party in the Society, in consequence of a burlesque poem which I gave in, as a candidate for the Literary Medal, entitled 'An Ode upon Nothing, with notes, by Trismegistus Rustifustius, D.D.' &c. For this squib against the great Dons of learning, the medal was voted to me by a triumphant majority. But a motion was made in the following week to rescind this vote; and a fierce contest between the two parties ensued, which I at last put an end to by voluntarily withdrawing my composition from the Society's Book.

I have already adverted to the period when Mr. Bunting's valuable volume first became known to me. There elapsed no very long time before I was myself the happy proprietor of a copy of the work, and, though never regularly instructed in music, could play over the airs with tolerable facility on the pianoforte. Robert Emmet used sometimes to sit by me, when I was thus engaged; and I remember one day his starting up as from a reverie, when I had just finished playing that spirited tune called the Red Fox,* and exclaiming, "Oh that I were at the head of twenty thousand men, marching to that air!"

How little did I then think that, in one of the most touching of the sweet airs I used to play to him, his own dying words would find an interpreter so worthy of their sad, but proud feeling;† or that another of those mournful strains ‡ would long be associated, in the hearts of his countrymen, with the memory of her ‖ who shared with Ireland his last blessing and prayer.

Though fully alive, of course, to the feelings which such music could not but inspire, I had not yet undertaken the task of adapting words to any of the airs; and it was, I am ashamed to say, in dull and turgid prose, that I made my first appearance in print as a champion of the popular cause. Towards the latter end of the year 1797, the celebrated newspaper called "The Press" was set up by Arthur O'Connor, Thomas Addis Emmet,

* " Let Erin remember the days of old."
† " Oh, breathe not his name."
‡ " She is far from the land where her young hero sleeps."
‖ Miss Curran.

and other chiefs of the United Irish conspiracy, with the view of preparing and ripening the public mind for the great crisis then fast approaching. This memorable journal, according to the impression I at present retain of it, was far more distinguished for earnestness of purpose and intrepidity, than for any great display of literary talent;—the bold letters written by Emmet (the elder), under the signature of "Montanus," being the only compositions I can now call to mind, as entitled to praise for their literary merit. It required, however, but a small sprinkling of talent to make bold writing, at that time, palatable; and, from the experience of my own home, I can answer for the avidity with which every line of this daring journal was devoured. It used to come out, I think, twice a week, and, on the evening of publication, I always read it aloud to our small circle after supper.

It may easily be conceived that, what with my ardour for the national cause, and a growing consciousness of some little turn for authorship, I was naturally eager to become a contributor to those patriotic and popular columns. But the constant anxiety about me which I knew my own family felt,—a feeling more wakeful far than even their zeal in the public cause—withheld me from hazarding any step that might cause them alarm. I had ventured, indeed, one evening, to pop privately into the letter-box of The Press, a short Fragment in imitation of Ossian. But this, though inserted, passed off quietly; and nobody was, in *any* sense of the phrase, the wiser for it. I was soon tempted, however, to try a more daring flight. Without communicating my secret to any one but Edward Hudson, I addressed a long Letter in prose to the ***** of ****, in which a profusion of bad flowers of rhetoric was enwreathed plentifully with that weed which Shakspeare calls "the cockle of rebellion," and, in the same manner as before, committed it tremblingly to the chances of the letter-box. I hardly expected my prose would be honoured with insertion, when, lo, on the next evening of publication, when, seated as usual in my little corner by the fire, I unfolded the paper for the purpose of reading it to my select auditory, there was my own Letter staring me full in the face, being honoured with so conspicuous a place as to be one of the first articles my audience would expect to hear. Assuming an outward appearance of ease, while every nerve within me was trembling, I contrived to accomplish the reading of the Letter without raising in either of my auditors a suspicion that it was my own. I enjoyed the pleasure too of hearing it a good deal praised by them; and might have been tempted by this to acknowledge myself the author, had I not found that the language and sentiments of the article were considered by both to be "very bold."*

---

* So thought also higher authorities; for, among the extracts from The Press brought forward by the Secret Committee of the House of Commons, to show how formidable had been the designs of the United

I was not destined, however, to remain long undetected. On the following day, Edward Hudson,† the only one, as I have said, entrusted with my secret, called to pay us a morning visit, and had not been long in the room, conversing with my mother, when looking significantly at me he said, 'Well, you saw ——' Here he stopped; but the mother's eye had followed his, with the rapidity of lightning, to mine, and at once she perceived the whole truth. "That Letter was yours, then?" she asked of me eagerly; and, without hesitation, of course, I acknowledged the fact; when in the most earnest manner she entreated of me never again to have any connexion with that paper; and, as every wish of hers was to me a law, I readily pledged the solemn promise she required. Though well aware how easily a sneer may be raised at the simple details of this domestic scene, I have yet ventured to put it on record, as affording an instance of the gentle and womanly watchfulness, —the providence, as it may be called, of the little world of home,—by which, although placed al-

---

Irishmen, there are two or three paragraphs cited from this redoubtable Letter.

† Of the depth and extent to which Hudson had involved himself in the conspiracy, none of our family had harboured the least notion : till, on the seizure of the thirteen Leinster delegates, at Oliver Bond's, in the month of March, 1798, we found, to our astonishment and sorrow, that he was one of the number.

To those unread in the painful history of this period, it is right to mention that almost all the leaders of the United Irish conspiracy were Protestants. Among those companions of my own alluded to in these pages, I scarcely remember a single Catholic.

most in the very current of so headlong a movement, and living familiarly with some of the most daring of those who propelled it, I yet was guarded from any participation in their secret oaths, counsels, or plans, and thus escaped all share in that wild struggle to which so many far better men than myself fell victims.

In the mean while, this great conspiracy was hastening on, with fearful precipitancy, to its outbreak; and vague and shapeless as are now known to have been the views even of those who were engaged practically in the plot, it is not any wonder that to the young and uninitiated like myself it should have opened prospects partaking far more of the wild dreams of poesy than of the plain and honest prose of real life. But a crisis was then fast approaching, when such self-delusions could no longer be indulged; and when the mystery which had hitherto hung over the plans of the conspirators was to be rent asunder by the stern hand of power.

Of the horrors that fore-ran and followed the frightful explosion of the year 1798, I have neither inclination nor, luckily, occasion to speak. But among those introductory scenes, which had somewhat prepared the public mind for such a catastrophe, there was one, of a painful description, which, as having been myself an actor in it, I may be allowed briefly to notice.

It was not many weeks, I think, before this crisis, that, owing to information gained by the college authorities of the rapid spread, among the students, not only of the principles but the organisation of the Irish Union,* a solemn visitation was held by Lord Clare, the vice-chancellor of the University, with the view of inquiring into the extent of this branch of the plot, and dealing summarily with those engaged in it.

Imperious and harsh as then seemed the policy of thus setting up a sort of inquisitorial tribunal, armed with the power of examining witnesses on oath, and in a place devoted to the instruction of youth, I cannot but confess that the facts which came out in the course of the evidence, went far towards justifying even this arbitrary proceeding; and to the many who, like myself, were acquainted only with the general views of the Union leaders, without even knowing, except from conjecture, who those leaders were, or what their plans or objects, it was most startling to hear the disclosures which every succeeding witness brought forth. There were a few, — and among that number, poor Robert Emmet, John Brown, and the two ＊＊＊＊＊＊ s ‡, whose total absence from the

* In the Report from the Secret Committee of the Irish House of Lords, this extension of the plot to the College is noticed as a " desperate project of the same faction to corrupt the youth of the country by introducing their organised system of treason into the University."

‡ One of these brothers had been long a general in the French army; having taken a part in all those great enterprises of Napoleon which have now become mater of history. Should these pages meet the eye of Gen. ＊＊＊＊＊, they will call to his mind the days we passed together in Normandy, a few summers since ;—more especially our excursion to Bayeux, when, as we talked on the way of old college times and friends

whole scene, as well as the dead silence that, day after day, followed the calling out of their names, proclaimed how deep had been their share in the unlawful proceedings inquired into by this tribunal.

But there was one young friend of mine, *******, whose appearance among the suspected and examined as much surprised as it deeply and painfully interested me. He and Emmet had long been intimate and attached friends;—their congenial fondness for mathematical studies having been, I think, a far more binding sympathy between them than any arising out of their political opinions. From his being called up, however, on this day, when, as it appeared afterwards, all the most important evidence was brought forward, there could be little doubt that, in addition to his intimacy with Emmet, the college authorities must have possessed some information which led them to suspect him of being an accomplice in the conspiracy. In the course of his examination, some questions were put to him which he refused to answer,—most probably from their tendency to involve or inculpate others; and he was accordingly dismissed, with the melancholy certainty that his future prospects in life were blasted; it being already known that the punishment for such contumacy was not merely expulsion from the University, but exclusion from all the learned professions.

all the eventful and stormy scenes we had passed through since seemed forgotten.

The proceedings, indeed of this whole day had been such as to send me to my home in the evening with no very agreeable feelings or prospects. I had heard evidence given affecting even the lives of some of those friends whom I had long regarded with admiration as well as affection; and what was still worse than even their danger,—a danger ennobled, I thought, by the cause in which they suffered,—was the shameful spectacle exhibited by those who had appeared in evidence against them. Of these witnesses, the greater number had been themselves involved in the plot, and now came forward either as voluntary informers, or else were driven by the fear of the consequences of refusal to secure their own safety at the expense of companions and friends.

I well remember the gloom, so unusual, that hung over our family circle on that evening, as, talking together of the events of the day, we discussed the likelihood of my being among those who would be called up for examination on the morrow. The deliberate conclusion, to which my dear honest advisers came, was that, overwhelming as the consequences were to all their plans and hopes for me, yet, if the questions leading to criminate others, which had been put to almost all examined on that day, and which poor ＊＊＊＊＊＊＊ alone had refused to answer, I must, in the same manner, and at all risks, return a similar refusal. I am not quite certain whether I received any intimation, on the following morning, that I was to be one of those examined in the course of the day; but I rather think some such notice had been conveyed to me;—and, at last, my awful turn came, and I stood in presence of the formidable tribunal. There sate, with severe look, the vice-chancellor, and, by his side, the memorable Doctor Duigenan, —memorable for his eternal pamphlets against the Catholics.

The oath was proffered to me. "I have an objection, my Lord," said I, "to taking this oath." "What is your objection?" he asked sternly. "I have no fears, my Lord, that any thing I might say would criminate myself; but it might tend to involve others, and I despise the character of the person who could be led, under any such circumstances, to inform against his associates." This was aimed at some of the revelations of the preceding day; and, as I learned afterwards, was so understood. "How old are you, Sir?" he then asked. "Between seventeen and eighteen, my Lord." He then turned to his assessor, Duigenan, and exchanged a few words with him, in an under tone of voice. "We cannot," he resumed, again addressing me, "suffer any one to remain in our University, who refuses to take this oath." "I shall, then, my Lord," I replied, "take the oath, —still reserving to myself the power of refusing to answer any such questions as I have just described." "We do not sit here to argue with *you*, Sir," he rejoined sharply; upon which I took the oath, and seated myself in the witnesses' chair.

The following are the questions and answers that then ensued. After adverting to the proved existence of United Irish Societies in the University, he asked, "Have you ever belonged to any of these societies?" "No, my Lord." "Have you ever known of any of the proceedings that took place in them?" "No, my Lord." "Did you ever hear of a proposal at any of their meetings, for the purchase of arms and ammunition?" "Never, my Lord." "Did you ever hear of a proposition made, in one of these societies, with respect to the expediency of assassination?" "Oh no, my Lord." He then turned again to Duigenan, and, after a few words with him, said to me:—"When such are the answers you are able to give*, pray what was the cause of your great repugnance to taking the oath?" "I have already told your Lordship my chief reason; in addition to which, it was the first oath I ever took, and the hesitation was, I think, natural."†

---

* There had been two questions put to all those examined on the first day,—"Were you ever asked to join any of these societies?"—and "By whom were you asked?"—which I should have refused to answer, and must, of course, have abided the consequences.

† For the correctness of the above report of this short examination, I can pretty confidently answer. It may amuse, therefore, my readers,—as showing the manner in which biographers make the most of small facts,—to see an extract or two from another account of this affair, published not many years since by an old and zealous friend of our family. After stating with tolerable correctness one or two of my answers, the writer thus proceeds:—"Upon this, Lord Clare repeated the question, and young Moore made such an appeal, as caused his lordship to relax, austere and rigid as he was. The words I cannot exactly remember; the substance was as follows:—that he entered college to receive the

I was now dismissed without any further questioning; and, however trying had been this short operation, was amply repaid for it by the kind zeal with which my young friends and companions flocked to congratulate me;—not so much, I was inclined to hope, on my acquittal by the court, as on the manner in which I had acquitted *myself*. Of my reception, on returning home, after the fears entertained of so very different a result, I will not attempt any description;—it was all that *such* a home alone could furnish.

I have been induced thus to continue down to the very verge of the warning outbreak of 1798, the slight sketch of my early days which I ventured to commence in the First Volume of this Collection: nor could I have furnished the Irish Melodies with any more pregnant illustration, as it was in those times, and among the events then stirring, that the feeling which afterwards found a voice in my country's music, was born and nurtured.

I shall now string together such detached notices and memoranda respecting this work, as I think may be likely to interest my readers.

education of a scholar and a gentleman; that he knew not how to compromise these characters by informing against his college companions; that his own speeches in the debating society had been ill construed, when the worst that could be said of them was, if truth had been spoken, that they were patriotic . . . that he was aware of the high-minded nobleman he had the honour of appealing to, and if his lordship could condescend to step from his high station and place himself in his situation, then say how he would act under such circumstances,—it would be his guidance."—HERBERT's Irish Varieties. London, 1836.

Of the few songs written with a concealed political feeling,—such as "When he who adores thee," and one or two more,—the most successful, in its day, was "When first I met thee warm and young," which alluded, in its hidden sense, to the Prince Regent's desertion of his political friends. It was little less, I own, than profanation to disturb the sentiment of so beautiful an air by any connexion with such a subject. The great success of this song, soon after I wrote it, among a large party staying at Chatsworth, is thus alluded to in one of Lord Byron's letters to me:—"I have heard from London that you have left Chatsworth and all there full of 'entusymusy' . . . . . . and, in particular, that 'When first I met thee' has been quite overwhelming in its effect. I told you it was one of the best things you ever wrote, though that dog * * * * wanted you to omit part of it."

It has been sometimes supposed that "Oh breathe not his name," was meant to allude to Lord Edward Fitzgerald: but this is a mistake; the song having been suggested by the well-known passage in Robert Emmet's dying speech, "Let no man write my epitaph . . . . . . let my tomb remain uninscribed, till other times and other men shall learn to do justice to my memory."

The feeble attempt to commemorate the glory of our great Duke—"When History's Muse," &c. —is in so far remarkable, that it made up amply for its want of poetical spirit, by an outpouring, rarely granted to bards in these days, of the spirit of prophecy. It was in the year 1815 that the following lines first made their appearance:—

> And still the last crown of thy toils is remaining,
>   The grandest, the purest, even THOU hast yet known;
> Though proud was thy task, other nations unchaining,
>   Far prouder to heal the deep wounds of thy own.
> At the foot of that throne, for whose weal thou hast stood.
>   Go, plead for the land that first cradled thy fame, &c.

About fourteen years after these lines were written, the Duke of Wellington recommended to the throne the great measure of Catholic Emancipation.

The fancy of the "Origin of the Irish Harp" was (as I have elsewhere acknowledged*) suggested by a drawing, made under peculiarly painful circumstances, by the friend so often mentioned in this sketch, Edward Hudson.

In connexion with another of these matchless airs,—one that defies all poetry to do it justice,—I find the following singular and touching statement in an article of the Quarterly Review. Speaking of a young and promising poetess, Lu-

---

* "When, in consequence of the compact entered into between government and the chief leaders of the conspiracy, the State Prisoners, before proceeding into exile, were allowed to see their friends, I paid a visit to Edward Hudson, in the jail of Kilmainham, where he had then lain immured for four or five months, hearing of friend after friend being led out to death, and expecting every week his own turn to come. I found that to amuse his solitude he had made a large drawing with charcoal on the wall of his prison, representing that fancied origin of the Irish Harp which, some years after, I adopted as the subject of one of the 'Melodies.'"— Life and Death of Lord Edward Fitzgerald, vol. i.

cretia Davidson, who died very early from nervous excitement, the Reviewer says, "She was particularly sensitive to music. There was one song (it was Moore's Farewell to his Harp) to which she took a special fancy. She wished to hear it only at twilight,—thus (with that same perilous love of excitement which made her place the Æolian harp in the window when she was composing), seeking to increase the effect which the song produced upon a nervous system, already diseasedly susceptible; for it is said that, whenever she heard this song, she became cold, pale, and almost fainting; yet it was her favourite of all songs, and gave occasion to those verses addressed in her fifteenth year to her sister."

With the Melody entitled, "Love, Valour, and Wit," an incident is connected, which awakened feelings in me of proud, but sad pleasure, to think that my songs had reached the hearts of some of the descendants of those great Irish families, who found themselves forced, in the dark days of persecution, to seek in other lands a refuge from the shame and ruin of their own;—those, whose story I have thus associated with one of their country's most characteristic airs:—

> Ye Blakes and O'Donnells, whose fathers resign'd
> The green hills of their youth, among strangers to find
> That repose which at home they had sigh'd for in vain.

From a foreign lady, of this ancient extraction, —whose names, could I venture to mention them, would lend to the incident an additional Irish charm,—I received about two years since, through the hands of a gentleman to whom it had been entrusted, a large portfolio, adorned inside with a beautiful drawing, representing Love, Wit, and Valour, as described in the song. In the border that surrounds the drawing are introduced the favourite emblems of Erin, the harp, the shamrock, the mitred head of St. Patrick, together with scrolls containing each, inscribed in letters of gold, the name of some favourite melody of the fair artist.

This present was accompanied by the following letter from the lady herself; and her Irish race, I fear, is but too discernible in the generous indiscretion with which, in this instance, she allows praise so much to outstrip desert:—

"*Le 25 Août*, 1836.

"Monsieur,

"Si les poëtes n'étoient en quelque sorte une propriété intellectuelle dont chacun prend sa part à raison de la puissance qu'ils exercent, je ne saurois en vérité comment faire pour justifier mon courage!—car il en falloit beaucoup pour avoir osé consacrer mon pauvre talent d'amateur à vos délicieuses poësies, et plus encore pour en renvoyer le pâle reflet à son véritable auteur.

"J'espère toutefois que ma sympathie pour l'Irlande vous fera juger ma foible production avec cette heureuse partialité qui impose silence à la critique: car, si je n'appartiens pas à l'Ile Verte par ma naissance, ni mes relations, je puis dire que je m'y intéresse avec un cœur Irlandais, et que j'ai conservé plus que le nom de mes pères. Cela seul me fait espérer que mes petits voyageurs ne subiront pas le triste noviciat des étrangers. Puissent-ils remplir leur mission sur le sol natal, en agissant conjointement et toujours pour la cause Irlandaise, et amener enfin une ére nouvelle pour cette héroïque et malheureuse nation:—le moyen de vaincre de tels adversaires s'ils ne font qu'un?

"Vous dirai-je, Monsieur, les doux moments que je dois á vos ouvrages? ce seroit répéter une fois de plus ce que vous entendez tous les jours et de tours les coins de la terre. Aussi j'ai garde de vous ravir un tems trop précieux par l'echo de ces vieilles vérités.

"Si jamais mon étoile me conduit en Irlande, je ne m'y croirai pas étrangére. Je sais que le passe y laisse de longs souvenirs, et que la conformité des désirs et des espérances rapproche en dépit de l'espace et du tems.

"Jusque-là, recevez, je vous prie, l'assurance de ma parfaite considération, avec laquelle j'ai l'honneur d'etre,

"Monsieur,
"Votre trés-humble servante,
"La Comtesse * * * * *"

Of the translations that have appeared of the Melodies in different languages, I shall here mention such as have come to my knowledge.

Latin.—"Cantus Hibernici," Nicholas Lee Torre, London, 1835.

Italian.—G. Flechia, Torino, 1836.—Adele Custi, Milano, 1836.

French.—Madame Belloc, Paris, 1823.—Loeve Veimars, Paris, 1829.

Russian.—Several detached Melodies, by the popular Russian poet Kozlof.

Polish.—Selections, in the same manner, by Niemcewich, Kosmian, and others.

I have now exhausted not so much my own recollections, as the patience, I fear, of my readers on this subject. We are told of painters calling those last touches of the pencil which they give to some favourite picture the "ultima basia;" and with the same sort of affectionate feeling do I now take leave of the Irish Melodies,—the only work of my pen, as I very sincerely believe, whose fame (thanks to the sweet music in which it is embalmed) may boast a chance of prolonging its existence to a day much beyond our own.

DEDICATION

TO

THE MARCHIONESS OF HEADFORT.

It is with a pleasure, not unmixed with melancholy, that I dedicate the last Number of the Irish Melodies to your Ladyship; nor can I have any doubt that the feelings with which you receive the tribute will be of the same mingled and saddened tone. To you, who, though but little beyond the season of childhood when the earlier numbers of this work appeared, lent the aid of your beautiful voice, and, even then, exquisite feeling for music, to the happy circle who met, to sing them together, under your father's roof, the gratification, whatever it may be, which this humble offering brings, cannot be otherwise than darkened by the mournful reflection, how many of the voices which then joined with ours are now silent in death!

I am not without hope that, as far as regards the grace and spirit of the Melodies, you will find this closing portion of the work not unworthy of what has preceded it. The Sixteen Airs, of which the Number and the Supplement consist, have been selected from the immense mass of Irish music which has been for years past accumulating in my hands; and it was from a desire to include all that appeared most worthy of preservation, that the four supplementary songs which follow the Tenth Number have been added.

Trusting that I may yet again, in remembrance of old times, hear our voices together in some of the harmonised airs of this Volume, I have the honour to subscribe myself,

Your Ladyship's faithful Friend and Servant,

THOMAS MOORE.

Sloperton Cottage,
May, 1834.

IRISH MELODIES.

IRISH MELODIES

IRISH MELODIES.

GO WHERE GLORY WAITS THEE.

Go where glory waits thee,
  But while fame elates thee,
    Oh still remember me!
When the praise thou meetest
To thine ear is sweetest,
  Oh then remember me!
Other arms may press thee,
Dearer friends caress thee,
All the joys that bless thee,
  Sweeter far may be;
But when friends are nearest,
And when joys are dearest,
  Oh then remember me!

When, at eve, thou rovest,
By the star thou lovest,
  Oh then remember me!
Think, when home returning,
Bright we've seen it burning
  Oh thus remember me!

Oft as summer closes,
When thine eye reposes
On its lingering roses,
　Once so lov'd by thee,
Think of her who wove them,
Her who made thee love them,
　Oh then remember me!

When, around thee dying,
Autumn leaves are lying,
　Oh then remember me!
And, at night, when gazing
On the gay hearth blazing,
　Oh still remember me!
Then should music, stealing
All the soul of feeling,
To thy heart appealing,
　Draw one tear from thee;
Then let memory bring thee
Strains I used to sing thee,—
　Oh then remember me!

WAR SONG.

REMEMBER THE GLORIES OF BRIEN THE BRAVE.

REMEMBER the glories of Brien the brave,*
　Though the days of the hero are o'er;
Though lost to Mononia,† and cold in the grave,
　He returns to Kinkora‡ no more.
That star of the field, which so often hath pour'd
　Its beam on the battle, is set;
But enough of its glory remains on each sword,
　To light us to victory yet.

Mononia! when Nature embellished the tint
　Of thy fields, and thy mountains so fair,
Did she ever intend that a tyrant should print
　The footstep of slavery there?
No! Freedom, whose smile we shall never resign,
　Go, tell our invaders, the Danes,
That 'tis sweeter to bleed for an age at thy shrine,
　Than to sleep but a moment in chains.

---

* Brien Borombe, the great monarch of Ireland, who was killed at the battle of Clontarf, in the beginning of the 11th century, after having defeated the Danes in twenty-five engagements.

† Munster　　　　　　　　‡ The palace of Brien.

Forget not our wounded companions, who stood*
  In the day of distress by our side;
While the moss of the valley grew red with their
      blood,
  They stirr'd not, but conquer'd and died.
That sun which now blesses our arms with his light
  Saw them fall upon Ossory's plain;—
Oh, let him not blush when he leaves us to-night,
  To find that they fell there in vain!

ERIN, THE TEAR AND THE SMILE.

ERIN! the tear and the smile in thine eyes,
  Blend like the rainbow that hangs in thy skies!
    Shining through sorrow's stream,
    Saddening through pleasure's beam,
    Thy suns with doubtful gleam
      Weep while they rise.

---

* This alludes to an interesting circumstance related of the Dalgais, the favorite troops of Brien, when they were interrupted in their return from the battle of Clontarf, by Fitzpatrick, prince of Ossory. The wounded men entreated that they might be allowed to fight with the rest. "Let stakes be stuck in the ground," said they, "and suffer each of us, tied to and supported by one of these stakes, to be placed in his rank by the side of a sound man."— "Between seven and eight hundred wounded men," adds O'Halloran, "pale, emaciated, and supported in this manner, appeared mixed with the foremost of the troops; never was such another sight exhibited." Hist. Ireland, bk. xii. chap. I.

Erin! thy silent tear never shall cease,
Erin! thy languid smile ne'er shall increase,
  Till, like the rainbow's light,
  Thy various tints unite,
  And form in heaven's sight
    One arch of peace!

O BREATHE NOT HIS NAME!

OH breathe not his name! let it sleep in the shade,
  Where cold and unhonor'd his relics are laid:
Sad, silent, and dark, be the tears that we shed,
As the night-dew that falls on the grass o'er his head.

But the night-dew that falls, tho' in silence it weeps,
Shall brighten with verdure the grave where he sleeps,
And the tear that we shed, though in secret it rolls,
Shall long keep his memory green in our souls.

WHEN HE WHO ADORES THEE.

WHEN he, who adores thee, has left but the name
    Of his fault and his sorrows behind,
Oh! say wilt thou weep, when they darken the fame
    Of a life that for thee was resigned?
Yes, weep, and however my foes may condemn,
    Thy tears shall efface their decree;
For Heaven can witness, though guilty to them,
    I have been but too faithful to thee.

With thee were the dreams of my earliest love;
  Every thought of my reason was thine;
In my last humble prayer to the Spirit above
  Thy name shall be mingled with mine.
Oh! blest are the lovers and friends who shall live
  The days of thy glory to see;
But the next dearest blessing that Heaven can give
  Is the pride of thus dying for thee.

THE HARP THAT ONCE THRO' TARA'S HALLS.

THE harp that once through Tara's halls
  The soul of music shed,
Now hangs as mute on Tara's walls,
  As if that soul were fled.—
So sleeps the pride of former days,
  So glory's chill is o'er;
And hearts, that once beat high for praise,
  Now feel that pulse no more.

No more to chiefs and ladies bright,
  The harp of Tara swells;
The chord alone, that breaks at night,
  Its tale of ruin tells.
Thus Freedom now so seldom wakes,
  The only throb she gives
Is when some heart indignant breaks,
  To show that still she lives.

FLY NOT YET.

Fly not yet, 'tis just the hour
   When pleasure, like the midnight flower,
That scorns the eye of vulgar light,
Begins to bloom for sons of night,
   And maids who love the moon.
'Twas but to bless these hours of shade
That beauty and the moon were made;
'Tis then their soft attractions glowing
Set the tides and goblets flowing.
   Oh stay! — Oh stay! —
Joy so seldom weaves a chain
Like this to-night, that O! 'tis pain
   To break its links so soon.

Fly not yet, the fount that play'd
In times of old through Ammon's shade,
Though icy cold by day it ran,
Yet still, like souls of mirth, began
   To burn when night was near.
And thus should woman's heart and looks
At noon be cold as winter brooks,
Nor kindle, till the night, returning,
Brings their genial hour for burning.
   Oh stay! — Oh stay! —
When did morning ever break,
And find such beaming eyes awake
   As those that sparkle here?

* Solis Fons, near the Temple of Ammon.

O, THINK NOT MY SPIRITS ARE ALWAYS AS LIGHT.

OH! think not my spirits are always as light,
  And as free from a pang, as they seem to you now;
Nor expect that the heart-beaming smile of to-night
  Will return with to-morrow to brighten my brow.
No:—life is a waste of wearisome hours,
  Which seldom the rose of enjoyment adorns;
And the heart that is soonest awake to the flowers
  Is always the first to be touched by the thorns.
But send round the bowl, and be happy awhile:—
  May we never meet worse, in our pilgrimage here,
Than the tear that enjoyment can gild with a smile,
  And the smile that compassion can turn to a tear.

The thread of our life would be dark, Heaven knows!
  If it were not with friendship and love intertwin'd;
And I care not how soon I may sink to repose,
  When these blessings shall cease to be dear to my mind.
But they who have lov'd the fondest, the purest,
  Too often have wept o'er the dream they believ'd;
And the heart that has slumber'd in friendship securest
  Is happy indeed if 'twas never deceiv'd.
But send round the bowl: while a relic of truth
  Is in man or in woman, this prayer shall be mine:
That the sunshine of love may illumine our youth,
  And the moonlight of friendship console our decline.

THOUGH THE LAST GLIMPSE OF ERIN.

THO' the last glimpse of Erin with sorrow I see,
  Yet wherever thou art shall seem Erin to me;
In exile thy bosom shall still be my home,
  And thine eyes make my climate wherever we roam.

To the gloom of some desert or cold rocky shore,
Where the eye of the stranger can haunt us no more,
I will fly with my Coulin, and think the rough wind
Less rude than the foes we leave frowning behind.

And I'll gaze on thy gold hair as graceful it wreathes,
And hang o'er thy soft harp as wildly it breathes;
Nor dread that the cold-hearted Saxon will tear
One chord from that harp, or one lock from that hair.*

---

* "In the twenty-eighth year of the reign of Henry VIII. an act was made respecting the habits and dress in general of the Irish, whereby all persons were restrained from being shorn or shaven above the ears, or from wearing Glibbes or Coulins, (long locks) on their heads, or hair on their upper lip, called Crommeal. On this occasion a song was written by one of our bards, in which an Irish virgin is made to give the preference to her dear Coulin, or the youth with the flowing locks, to all strangers (by which the English were meant,) or those who wore their habits. Of this song, the air alone has reached us, and is universally admired.
  Walker's Historical Memoirs of Irish Bards.
  Mr. Walker informs us also, that about the same period, there were some harsh measures taken against the Irish minstrels.

RICH AND RARE WERE THE GEMS.

RICH and rare were the gems she wore,*
And a bright gold ring on her wand she bore;
But oh! her beauty was far beyond
Her sparkling gems, or snow-white wand.

"Lady! dost thou not fear to stray
"So lone and lovely through this bleak way?
"Are Erin's sons so good or so cold,
"As not to be tempted by woman or gold?"

"Sir Knight! I feel not the least alarm,
"No son of Erin will offer me harm:—
"For, though they love woman and golden store,
"Sir Knight! they love honor and virtue more."

On she went, and her maiden smile
In safety lighted her round the green isle;
And blest for ever is she who relied
Upon Erin's honor and Erin's pride.

---

* This ballad is founded upon the following anecdote.—"The people were inspired with such a spirit of honor, virtue and religion, by the great example of Brien, and by his excellent administration, that, as a proof of it, we are informed that a young lady of great beauty, adorned with jewels and a costly dress, undertook a journey alone from one end of the kingdom to the other, with a wand only in her hand, at the top of which was a ring of exceeding great value; and such an impression had the laws and government of this monarch made on the minds of all the people, that no attempt was made upon her honor, nor was she robbed of her clothes or jewels." Warner's Hist. Ireland, vol i. book x.

AS A BEAM O'ER THE FACE OF THE WATERS.

As a beam o'er the face of the waters may glow,
　　While the tide runs in darkness and coldness below,
So the cheek may be ting'd with a warm sunny smile,
Though the cold heart to ruin runs darkly the while.

One fatal remembrance, one sorrow that throws
Its bleak shades alike o'er our joys and our woes,
To which life nothing darker or brighter can bring,
For which joy has no balm, and affliction no sting—

O! this thought in the midst of enjoyment will stay,
Like a dead leafless branch in the summer's bright ray;
The beams of the warm sun play round it in vain,
It may smile in his light, but it blooms not again.

THE MEETING OF THE WATERS.*

There is not in the wide world a valley so sweet,
　　As that vale in whose bosom the bright waters meet; †
Oh! the last rays of feeling and life must depart,
Ere the bloom of that valley shall fade from my heart.

* "The meeting of the waters" forms a part of that beautiful scenery which lies between Rathdrum and Arklow, in the county of Wicklow, and these lines were suggested by a visit to this romantic spot in the summer of the year 1807.

† The rivers Avon and Avoca.

Yet it was not that nature had shed o'er the scene
Her purest of crystal and brightest of green;
'Twas not her soft magic of streamlet or hill,
Oh no!—it was something more exquisite still.

'Twas that friends, the belov'd of my bosom, were
    near,
Who made each dear scene of enchantment more dear,
And who felt how the best charms of nature improve,
When we see them reflected from looks that we love.

Sweet vale of Avoca! how calm could I rest
In thy bosom of shade with the friends I love best,
Where the storms that we feel in this cold world
    should cease,
And our hearts, like thy waters, be mingled in peace.

ST. SENANUS AND THE LADY.*

ST. SENANUS.

"OH! haste and leave this sacred isle,
    Unholy bark! ere morning smile,
For on thy deck, though dark it be,
    A female form I see;
And I have sworn this sainted sod
Shall ne'er by woman's feet be trod."

---

* In a metrical life of St. Senanus, which is taken from an old
Kilkenny MS. and may be found among the Acta Sanctorum Hi-
berniæ, we are told of his flight to the island of Scattery, and his

THE LADY.

"Oh Father ! send not hence my bark,
Through wintry winds and billows dark;
I come with humble heart to share
    Thy morn and evening prayer;
Nor mine the feet, O holy saint !
The brightness of thy sod to taint."

The Lady's prayer Senanus spurn'd,
The winds blew fresh, the bark return'd ;
But legends hint, that had the maid
    Till morning's light delay'd,
And given the saint one rosy smile,
She ne'er had left his lonely isle.

---

resolution not to admit any woman of the party. He refused to receive even a sister saint (St. Cannera) whom an angel had taken to the island, for the express purpose of introducing her to him. The following was the ungracious answer of Senanus, according to his poetical biographer :

> Cui Præsul, quid fœminis
> Commune est cum monachis ?
> Nec te nec ullam aliam
> Admittemus in insulam.

See the 'Acta Sanct. Hib.' p. 610.

According to Dr. Ledwich, St. Senanus was no less a personage than the river Shannon, but O'Connor and other antiquarians deny the metamorphose indignantly.

HOW DEAR TO ME THE HOUR.

HOW dear to me the hour when daylight dies,
  And sunbeams melt along the silent sea!
For then sweet dreams of other days arise,
  And memory breathes her vesper sigh to thee.

And, as I watch the line of light, that plays
  Along the smooth wave toward the burning west,
I long to tread that golden path of rays,
  And think 'twould lead to some bright isle of rest.

TAKE BACK THE VIRGIN PAGE.

WRITTEN ON RETURNING A BLANK BOOK.

TAKE back the virgin page,
  White and unwritten still;
Some hand more calm and sage
  The leaf must fill.
Thoughts come as pure as light,
  Pure as even *you* require;
But oh! each word I write
  Love turns to fire.

Yet let me keep the book:
  Oft shall my heart renew,
When on its leaves I look,
  Dear thoughts of you.
Like you 'tis fair and bright;
  Like you too bright and fair
To let wild passion write
  One wrong wish there.

Haply, when from those eyes
　Far, far away I roam,
Should calmer thoughts arise
　Towards you and home;
Fancy may trace some line
　Worthy those eyes to meet;
Thoughts that not burn, but shine,
　Pure, calm, and sweet.

And as, o'er ocean far,
　Seamen their records keep,
Led by some hidden star
　Through the cold deep;
So may the words I write
　Tell through what storms I stray—
You still the unseen light
　Guiding my way.

THE LEGACY.

WHEN in death I shall calm recline,
　O bear my heart to my mistress dear;
Tell her it liv'd upon smiles and wine
　Of the brightest hue, while it linger'd here.
Bid her not shed one tear of sorrow,
　To sully a heart so brilliant and light;
But balmy drops of the red grape borrow,
　To bathe the relic from morn till night.

When the light of my song is o'er,
　Then take my harp to your ancient hall;
Hang it up at that friendly door
　Where weary travellers love to call.*
Then if some bard, who roams forsaken,
　Revive its soft note in passing along,
Oh! let one thought of its master waken
　Your warmest smile for the child of song.

Keep this cup, which is now o'erflowing,
　To grace your revel when I'm at rest;
Never, O never its balm bestowing
　On lips that beauty hath seldom blest.
But when some warm devoted lover
　To her he adores shall bathe its brim,
Then, then my spirit around shall hover,
　And hallow each drop that foams for him.

HOW OFT HAS THE BENSHEE CRIED.

HOW oft has the Benshee cried,
　How oft has death untied
　　Bright links that Glory wove,
　　Sweet bonds entwined by Love!
Peace to each manly soul that sleepeth!
Rest to each faithful eye that weepeth!
　　Long may the fair and brave
　　Sigh o'er the hero's grave!

---

* "In every house was one or two harps, free to all travellers, who were the more caressed the more they excelled in music."—O'HALLORAN.

We're fallen upon gloomy days!*
Star after star decays,
Every bright name that shed
Light o'er the land is fled.
Dark falls the tear of him who mourneth
Lost joy, or hope that ne'er returneth:
But brightly flows the tear
Wept o'er a hero's bier.

Quench'd are our beacon lights —
Thou of the Hundred Fights!†
Thou, on whose burning tongue
Truth, peace, and freedom hung!‡
Both mute, — but long as valor shineth,
Or mercy's soul at war repineth,
So long shall Erin's pride
Tell how they liv'd and died.

* I have endeavored here, without losing that Irish character which it is my object to preserve throughout this work, to allude to the sad and ominous fatality, by which England has been deprived of so many great and good men, at a moment when she most requires all the aids of talent and integrity.

† This designation, which has been applied to Lord Nelson before, is the title given to a celebrated Irish Hero, in a Poem by O'Guive, the bard of O'Niel, which is quoted in the "Philosophical Survey of the South of Ireland," page 433. "Con of the Hundred fights, sleep in thy grass-grown tomb, and upbraid not our defeats with thy victories!"

‡ Fox, "Romanorum ultimus."

WE MAY ROAM THRO' THIS WORLD.

WE may roam through this world, like a child
　　at a feast,
　Who but sips of a sweet, and then flies to the rest
And when pleasure begins to grow dull in the east,
　We may order our wings and be off to the west;
But if hearts that feel, and eyes that smile,
　Are the dearest gifts that Heaven supplies,
We never need leave our own green isle
　For sensitive hearts and for sun-bright eyes.
Then remember, wherever your goblet is crown'd,
　　Through this world, whether eastward or west-
　　　　ward you roam,
When a cup to the smile of dear woman goes round,
　O remember the smile that adorns her at home.

In England the garden of beauty is kept
　By a dragon of prudery placed within call;
But so oft this unamiable dragon has slept,
　That the garden's but carelessly watch'd after all.
O they want the wild sweet-briery fence,
　Which round the flowers of Erin dwells;
Which warns the touch, while winning the sense,
　Nor charms us least when it most repels.
Then remember, wherever your goblet is crown'd,
　　Through this world, whether eastward or west-
　　　　ward you roam,
When a cup to the smile of dear woman goes round,
　O remember the smile that adorns her at home.

In France, when the heart of a woman sets sail,
  On the ocean of wedlock its fortune to try,
Love seldom goes far in a vessel so frail,
  But just pilots her off, and then bids her good-bye!
While the daughters of Erin keep the boy
  Ever smiling beside his faithful oar,
Through billows of woe, and beams of joy,
  The same as he look'd when he left the shore.
Then remember, wherever your goblet is crown'd,
  Through this world, whether eastward or westward you roam,
When a cup to the smile of dear woman goes round,
  O remember the smile that adorns her at home.

EVELEEN'S BOWER.

O WEEP for the hour
    When to Eveleen's bower
The Lord of the Valley with false vows came!
    The moon hid her light
    From the heavens that night,
And wept behind the clouds o'er the maiden's shame.

    The clouds pass'd soon
    From the chaste cold moon,
And heaven smiled again with her vestal flame;
    But none will see the day
    When the clouds shall pass away,
Which that dark hour left upon Eveleen's fame.

The white snow lay
On the narrow path-way,
When the Lord of the Valley cross'd over tne moor;
And many a deep print
On the white snow's tint
Show'd the track of his footstep to Eveleen's door.

The next sun's ray
Soon melted away
Every trace on the path where the false Lord came;
But there's a light above,
Which alone can remove
That stain upon the snow of fair Eveleen's fame.

LET ERIN REMEMBER.

LET Erin remember the days of old,
  Ere her faithless sons betrayed her;
When Malachi wore the collar of gold,*
  Which he won from her proud invader.
When her kings, with standard of green unfurled,
  Led the Red-Branch Knights to danger;—†
Ere the emerald gem of the western world
  Was set in the crown of a stranger.

---

* " This brought on an encounter between Malachi (the monarch of Ireland in the 10th century) and the Danes, in which Malachi defeated two of their champions, whom he encountered successively, hand to hand, taking a collar of gold from the neck of one, and carrying off the sword of the other, as trophies of his victory.—WARNER's Hist. Ireland, vol. i. bk. 9.

† " Military orders of knights were very early established in

On Lough Neagh's bank, as the fisherman strays,
  When the clear cold eve's declining,
He sees the round towers of other days
  In the wave beneath him shining;
Thus shall memory often, in dreams sublime,
  Catch a glimpse of the days that are over;
Thus, sighing, look through the waves of time,
  For the long-faded glories they cover.*

Ireland. Long before the birth of Christ we find an hereditary order of chivalry in Ulster, called Curaidhe na Craiobhe ruadh, or 'the Knights of the Red Branch,' from their chief seat in Emania, adjoining to the palace of the Ulster kings, called Teagh na Craiobhe ruadh, or the Academy of the Red Branch; and contiguous to which was a large hospital, founded for the sick knights and soldiers, called Bron-bhearg, or the House of the Sorrowful Soldier."—O'Halloran's Introduction, part i. chap. v.

* It was an old tradition, in the time of Giraldus, that Lough Neagh had been originally a fountain, by whose sudden overflowing the country was inundated, and a whole region, like the Atlantis of Plato, overwhelmed. He says that the fishermen in clear weather used to point out to strangers the tall ecclesiastical towers under water. 'Piscatores aquæ illius turres ecclesiasticas, quæ more patriæ arctæ sunt et altæ, necnon et rotundæ, sub undis manifeste, sereno tempore conspiciunt, et extraneis, transeuntibus, reique causas admirantibus frequenter ostendunt.'—Topo. Hib. Dist.

THE SONG OF FIONNUALA.*

SILENT, O Moyle! be the roar of thy water,
  Break not, ye breezes, your chain of repose!
While, murmuring mournfully, Lir's lonely daughter
  Tells to the night-star her tale of woes.
When shall the swan, her death-note singing,
  Sleep with wings in darkness furled?
When will heaven, its sweet bell ringing,
  Call my spirit from this stormy world?

Sadly, O Moyle, to thy winter-wave weeping,
  Fate bids me languish long ages away;
Yet still in her darkness doth Erin lie sleeping,
  Still doth the pure light its dawning delay.
When will that day-star, mildly springing,
  Warm our isle with peace and love?
When will heaven, its sweet bell ringing,
  Call my spirit to the fields above?

* To make this story intelligible in a song, would require a much greater number of verses than any one is authorised to inflict upon an audience at once; the reader must therefore be content to learn, in a note, that Fionnuala, the daughter of Lir, was by some supernatural power transformed into a swan, and condemned to wander, for many hundred years, over certain lakes and rivers in Ireland, till the coming of Christianity; when the first sound of the mass bell was to be the signal of her release. I found this fanciful fiction among some manuscript translations from the Irish, which were begun under the direction of that enlightened friend of Ireland, the late Countess of Moira.

COME SEND ROUND THE WINE.

COME, send round the wine, and leave points of belief
  To simpleton sages, and reasoning fools;
This moment's a flower too fair and brief
  To be wither'd and stain'd by the dust of the schools.
Your glass may be purple, and mine may be blue,
  But while they're fill'd from the same bright bowl,
The fool, who would quarrel for difference of hue,
  Deserves not the comfort they shed o'er the soul.

Shall I ask the brave soldier who fights by my side
  In the cause of mankind, if our creeds agree?
Shall I give up the friend I have valued and tried,
  If he kneel not before the same altar with me?
From the heretic girl of my soul should I fly,
  To seek somewhere else a more orthodox kiss?
No, perish the hearts and the laws that try
  Truth, valour, or love, by a standard like this!

SUBLIME WAS THE WARNING.

SUBLIME was the warning that Liberty spoke,
  And grand was the moment when Spaniards awoke
Into life and revenge from the conqueror's chain.
O Liberty!—let not this spirit have rest
Till it move, like a breeze, o'er the waves of the west;

Give the light of your look to each sorrowing spot,
Nor O, be the Shamrock of Erin forgot,
   While you add to your garland the Olive of Spain.

If the fame of our fathers, bequeath'd with their rights,
Give to country its charm, and to home its delights,
   If deceit be a wound, and suspicion a stain,
Then, ye men of Iberia, our cause is the same.
And O may his tomb want a tear and a name,
Who would ask for a nobler, a holier death,
Than to turn his last sigh into victory's breath,
   For the Shamrock of Erin and Olive of Spain!

Ye Blakes and O'Donnels, whose fathers resign'd
The green hills of their youth, among strangers to find
   That repose which, at home, they had sighed for in vain,
Join, join in our hope, that the flame which you light
May be felt yet in Erin, as calm and as bright,
And forgive even Albion, while blushing she draws,
Like a truant, her sword in the long-slighted cause
   Of the Shamrock of Erin and Olive of Spain!

God prosper the cause!—O, it cannot but thrive,
While the pulse of one patriot heart is alive,
   Its devotion to feel, and its rights to maintain.
Then how sainted by sorrow its martyrs will die!
The finger of Glory shall point where they lie;
While, far from the footstep of coward or slave,
The young spirit of Freedom shall shelter their grave
   Beneath Shamrocks of Erin and Olives of Spain!

BELIEVE ME, IF ALL THOSE ENDEARING.

Believe me, if all those endearing young charms,
  Which I gaze on so fondly to-day,
Were to change by to-morrow, and fleet in my arms,
  Like fairy gifts, fading away;
Thou wouldst still be ador'd, as this moment thou art,
  Let thy loveliness fade as it will;
And around the dear ruin each wish of my heart
  Would entwine itself verdantly still.

It is not while beauty and youth are thine own,
  And thy cheeks unprofan'd by a tear,
That the fervor and faith of a soul can be known,
  To which time will but make thee more dear.
No, the heart that has truly lov'd never forgets,
  But as truly loves on to the close!
As the sun-flower turns on her god, when he sets,
  The same look which she turn'd when he rose.

ERIN, OH ERIN.

LIKE the bright lamp that shone in Kildare's holy fane,*
  And burn'd thro' long ages of darkness and storm,
Is the heart that sorrows have frown'd on in vain,
  Whose spirit outlives them unfading and warm.
Erin, O Erin, thus bright through the tears
Of a long night of bondage thy spirit appears!

The nations have fallen and thou still art young,
  Thy sun is but rising, when others are set;
And tho' slavery's cloud o'er thy morning hath hung,
  The full noon of freedom shall beam round thee yet.
Erin, O Erin, though long in the shade,
Thy star will shine out when the proudest shall fade.

Unchill'd by the rain, and unwak'd by the wind,
  The lily lies sleeping thro' winter's cold hour,
Till Spring's light touch her fetters unbind,
  And daylight and liberty bless the young flower.†
Erin, O Erin, *thy* winter is past,
And the hope that liv'd thro' it shall blossom at last.

---

* The inextinguishable fire of St. Bridget, at Kildare, which Giraldus mentions, "Apud Kildariam occurrit Ignis Sanctæ Brigidæ quem inextinguibilem vocant; non quod extingui non possit, sed quod tam solicite moniales et sanctæ mulieres ignem, suppetente materia, fovent et nutriunt, ut a tempore virginis per tot annorum curricula semper mansit inextinctus."—GIRALD. Cam. de Mirabil. Hibern. dist. ii. c. 34.

† Mrs. H. Tighe, in her exquisite lines on the lily, has applied this image to a still more important object.

DRINK TO HER.

DRINK to her who long
    Hath wak'd the poet's sigh,
The girl who gave to song
    What gold could never buy.
Oh! woman's heart was made,
    For minstrel hands alone;
By other fingers play'd
    It yields not half the tone.
Then here's to her who long
    Hath wak'd the poet's sigh,
The girl who gave to song
    What gold could never buy.

At Beauty's door of glass,
    When Wealth and Wit once stood,
They ask'd her "which might pass?"
    She answer'd, "he who could."
With golden key Wealth thought
    To pass — but 'twould not do;
While Wit a diamond brought,
    Which cut his bright way through.
So here's to her who long
    Hath wak'd the poet's sigh,
The girl who gave to song
    What gold could never buy.

The love that seeks a home
    Where wealth or grandeur shines,
Is like the gloomy gnome
    That dwells in dark gold mines.

But O, the poet's love
  Can boast a brighter sphere;
Its native home 's above,
  Though woman keeps it here.
Then drink to her who long
  Hath wak'd the poet's sigh,
The girl who gave to song
  What gold could never buy.

O BLAME NOT THE BARD.*

OH! blame not the bard, if he fly to the bowers,
  Where pleasure lies carelessly smiling at fame;
He was born for much more, and in happier hours
  His soul might have burn'd with a holier flame.
The string, that now languishes loose o'er the lyre,
  Might have bent a proud bow to the warrior's dart,†
And the lip, which now breathes but the song of desire,
  Might have pour'd the full tide of a patriot's heart.

But alas for his country! — her pride is gone by,
  And that spirit is broken, which never would bend;

---

* We may suppose this apology to have been uttered by one of those wandering bards, whom Spenser so severely, and perhaps truly, describes in his 'State of Ireland,' and whose poems, he tells us, 'were sprinkled with some pretty flowers of their natural device, which have good grace and comeliness unto them, the which it is great pity to see abused to the gracing of wickedness and vice, which, with good usage, would serve to adorn and beautify virtue.'

† It is conjectured by Wormius, that the name of Ireland is derived from YR, the Runic for a Bow, in the use of which weapon the Irish were once very expert. This derivation is certainly more creditable to us than the following: "So that Ireland (called the land of IRE, for the constant broils therein for 400 years) was now become the land of concord.—LLOYD's State Worthies.

O'er the ruin her children in secret must sigh,
  For 'tis treason to love her, and death to defend.
Unpriz'd are her sons till they've learn'd to betray;
  Undistinguish'd they live, if they shame not their sires,
And the torch that would light them through dignity's way
  Must be caught from the pile where their country expires.

Then blame not the bard, if in pleasure's soft dream
  He should try to forget what he never can heal;
O give but a hope! — let a vista but gleam
  Through the gloom of his country, and mark how he'll feel!
That instant, his heart at her shrine would lay down
  Every passion it nurs'd, every bliss it ador'd,
While the myrtle, now idly entwin'd with his crown,
  Like the wreath of Harmodius, should cover his sword.*

But tho' glory be gone, and tho' hope fade away,
  Thy name, lov'd Erin, shall live in his songs!
Not ev'n in the hour, when his heart is most gay,
  Will he lose the remembrance of thee and thy wrongs.
The stranger shall hear thy lament on his plains;
  The sigh of thy harp shall be sent o'er the deep,
Till thy masters themselves, as they rivet thy chains,
  Shall pause at the song of their captive, and weep!

* See the hymn attributed to Alcæus, Εν μυρτου κλαδι το ξιφος φορησω—'I will carry my sword hidden in myrtles, like Harmodius and Aristogiton,' &c.

WHILE GAZING ON THE MOON'S LIGHT.

WHILE gazing on the moon's light,
    A moment from her smile I turn'd,
To look at orbs, that, more bright,
    In lone and distant glory burn'd.
        But *too* far
        Each proud star,
For me to feel its warming flame;
        Much more dear
        That mild sphere,
Which near our planet smiling came; *
Thus, Mary, be but thou my own;
    While brighter eyes unheeded play,
I'll love those moonlight looks alone,
    That bless my home and guide my way.

The day had sunk in dim showers,
    But midnight now, with lustre meek,
Illumin'd all the pale flowers,
    Like hope upon a mourner's cheek.
        I said (while
        The moon's smile

---

* "Of such celestial bodies as are visible, the sun excepted, the single moon, as despicable as it is in comparison to most of the others, is much more beneficial than they all put together."—WHISTON's Theory, &c.

In the 'Entretiens d'Ariste,' among other ingenious emblems, we find a starry sky without a moon, with these words 'Non mille, quod absens.'

Play'd o'er a stream, in dimpling bliss),
"The moon looks
"On many brooks,
"The brook can see no moon but this."*
And thus I thought our fortunes run,
For many a lover looks to thee,
While O, I feel there is but *one*,
One Mary in the world for me.

ILL OMENS.

WHEN daylight was yet sleeping under the billow,
And stars in the heavens still lingering shone,
Young Kitty, all blushing, rose up from her pillow,
The last time she e'er was to press it alone.
For the youth whom she treasur'd her heart and her soul in
Had promis'd to link the last tie before noon;
And when once the young heart of a maiden is stolen,
The maiden herself will steal after it soon.

As she look'd in the glass, which a woman ne'er misses,
Nor ever wants time for a sly glance or two,
A butterfly, fresh from the night-flower's kisses, †
Flew over the mirror, and shaded her view.

---

* This image was suggested by the following thought, which occurs somewhere in Sir William Jones's works: "The moon looks upon many night-flowers, the night-flower sees but one moon."

† An emblem of the soul.

Enrag'd with the insect for hiding her graces,
  She brush'd him — he fell, alas, never to rise !—
"Ah! such," said the girl, "is the pride of our faces,
  For which the soul's innocence too often dies."

While she stole through the garden where heart's-ease was growing,
  She cull'd some, and kiss'd off its night-fallen dew;
And a rose, further on, look'd so tempting and glowing,
  That, spite of her haste, she must gather it too.
But while o'er the roses too carelessly leaning,
  Her zone flew in two, and the heart's-ease was lost;
"Ah! this means," said the girl, (and she sigh'd at its meaning,)
  "That love is scarce worth the repose it will cost."

BEFORE THE BATTLE.

BY the hope within us springing,
  Herald of to-morrow's strife,
By that sun, whose light is bringing
  Chains or freedom, death or life —
Oh! remember, life can be
No charm for him who lives not free!
  Like the day-star in the wave
  Sinks a hero in his grave,
'Midst the dew-fall of a nation's tears.

Happy is he o'er whose decline
    The smiles of home may soothing shine,
And light him down the steep of years;—
    But O, how blest they sink to rest,
    Who close their eyes on victory's breast!

O'er his watch-fire's fading embers
    Now the foeman's cheek turns white
When his heart that field remembers,
    Where we tam'd his tyrant might!
Never let him bind again
A chain like that we broke from then.
    Hark! the horn of combat calls —
    Ere the golden evening falls
May we pledge that horn in triumph round.*
    Many a heart that now beats high,
    In slumber cold at night shall lie,
Nor waken ev'n at victory's sound:—
    But O, how blest that hero's sleep,
    O'er whom a wondering world shall weep!

AFTER THE BATTLE.

NIGHT clos'd around the conqueror's way,
    And lightnings show'd the distant hill,
Where those who lost that dreadful day
    Stood few and faint, but fearless still!

* "The Irish corna was not entirely devoted to martial purposes. In the heroic ages, our ancestors quaffed meadh out of them, as the Danish hunters do their beverage at this day.—WALKER.

The soldier's hope, the patriot's zeal,
    For ever dimm'd, for ever cross'd —
Oh! who shall say what heroes feel,
    When all but life and honor's lost?

The last sad hour of freedom's dream,
    And valor's task, mov'd slowly by,
While mute they watch'd, till morning's beam
    Should rise, and give them light to die.
There's yet a world where souls are free,
    Where tyrants taint not nature's bliss;
If death that world's bright opening be,
    Oh! who would live a slave in this?

'TIS SWEET TO THINK.

'TIS sweet to think, that, where'er we rove,
    We are sure to find something blissful and dear,
And that when we're far from the lips we love,
    We've but to make love to the lips we are near.*

---

* I believe it is Marmontel who says, 'Quand on n'a pas ce que l'on aime, il faut aimer ce que l'on a.'—There are so many matter-of-fact people, who take such jeux d'esprit as this defence of inconstancy, to be the actual and genuine sentiments of him who writes them, that they compel one in self-defence to be as matter-of-fact as themselves, and to remind them that Democritus was not the worse physiologist, for having playfully contended that snow was black; nor Erasmus in any degree the less wise for having written an ingenious encomium on folly.

The heart, like a tendril, accustom'd to cling,
   Let it grow where it will, cannot flourish alone,
But will lean to the nearest and loveliest thing
   It can twine with itself, and make closely its own.
Then O what pleasure, where'er we rove,
   To be sure to find something, still, that is dear,
And to know when far from the lips we love,
   We've but to make love to the lips we are near.

'Twere a shame, when flowers around us rise,
   To make light of the rest, if the rose is n't there;
And the world so rich in resplendent eyes,
   'Twere a pity to limit one's love to a pair.
Love's wing and the peacock's are nearly alike,
   They are both of them bright, but they're changeable too,
And, wherever a new beam of beauty can strike,
   It will tincture Love's plume with a different hue!
Then O what pleasure, where'er we rove,
   To be sure to find something, still, that is dear,
And to know, when far from the lips we love,
   We've but to make love to the lips we are near.

THE IRISH PEASANT TO HIS MISTRESS.*

THROUGH grief and through danger thy smile hath cheer'd my way,
Till hope seem to bud from each thorn that round me lay;

* Meaning, allegorically, the ancient Church of Ireland.

The darker our fortune, the brighter our pure love burn'd,
Till shame into glory, till fear into zeal was turn'd.
Yes, slave as I was, in thy arms my spirit felt free,
And bless'd ev'n the sorrows that made me more dear to thee.

Thy rival was honor'd, while thou wert wrong'd and scorn'd,
Thy crown was of briers, while gold her brows adorn'd;
She woo'd me to temples, while thou lay'st hid in caves,
Her friends were all masters, while thine, alas, were slaves;
Yet cold in the earth at thy feet I would rather be,
Than wed what I love not, or turn one thought from thee.

They slander thee sorely, who say thy vows are frail;
Hadst thou been a false one thy cheek had look'd less pale!
They say too, so long thou hast worn those lingering chains,
That deep in thy heart they have printed their servile stains —
O, foul is the slander! — no chain could that soul subdue —
Where shineth *thy* spirit, there liberty shineth too.*

---

* "Where the spirit of the Lord is, there is liberty."—St Paul, 2 Cor. iii. 17.

ON MUSIC.

WHEN through life unblest we rove,
    Losing all that made life dear,
Should some notes we us'd to love
    In days of boyhood meet our ear,
O how welcome breathes the strain!
    Wakening thoughts that long have slept,
Kindling former smiles again
    In faded eyes that long have wept.

Like the gale that sighs along
    Beds of oriental flowers,
Is the grateful breath of song,
    That once was heard in happier hours;
Fill'd with balm the gale sighs on,
    Though the flowers have sunk in death;
So when pleasure's dream is gone,
    Its memory lives in Music's breath.

Music! O how faint, how weak,
    Language fades before thy spell!
Why should Feeling ever speak
    When thou canst breathe her soul so well?
Friendship's balmy words may feign,
    Love's are ev'n more false than they;
Oh 'tis only Music's strain
    Can sweetly soothe and not betray.

IT IS NOT THE TEAR.

IT is not the tear at this moment shed,*
   When the cold turf has just been lain o'er him,
That can tell how belov'd was the friend that's fled,
   Or how deep in our hearts we deplore him.
'Tis the tear through many a long day wept,
   'Tis life's whole path o'ershaded;
'Tis the one remembrance fondly kept,
   When all lighter griefs are faded.

Thus his memory, like some holy light,
   Kept alive in our hearts, will improve them;
For worth shall look fairer, and truth more bright,
   When we think how he liv'd but to love them!
And as fresher flowers the sod perfume
   Where buried saints are lying,
So our hearts shall borrow a sweetening bloom
   From the image he left there in dying!

THE ORIGIN OF THE HARP.

'TIS believ'd that this Harp, which I wake now for thee,
Was a Siren of old, who sung under the sea,
And who often, at eve, thro' the bright waters rov'd,
To meet on the green shore a youth whom she lov'd.

---

* These lines were occasioned by the loss of a very near and dear relative, who died at Madeira.

But she lov'd him in vain, for he left her to weep,
And in tears, all the night, her gold tresses to steep,
Till Heaven look'd with pity on true love so warm,
And chang'd to this soft Harp the sea-maiden's form.

Still her bosom rose fair — still her cheeks smil'd
    the same —
While her sea-beauties gracefully formed the light
    frame;
And her hair, as, let loose, o'er her white arm it fell,
Was chang'd to bright chords uttering melody's spell.

Hence it came that this soft Harp so long hath been
    known
To mingle love's language with sorrow's sad tone;
Till *thou* didst divide them, and teach the fond lay
To speak love when I'm near thee, and grief when
    away.

LOVE'S YOUNG DREAM.

OH! the days are gone, when Beauty bright
    My heart's chain wove;
When my dream of life, from morn till night,
    Was love, still love!
        New hope may bloom,
        And days may come,
    Of milder, calmer beam,

But there's nothing half so sweet in life
  As love's young dream:
No, there's nothing half so sweet in life
  As love's young dream.

Though the bard to purer fame may soar,
  When wild youth's past;
Though he win the wise, who frown'd before,
  To smile at last;
  He'll never meet
  A joy so sweet,
  In all his noon of fame,
As when first he sung to woman's ear
  His soul-felt flame,
And, at every close, she blush'd to hear
  The one lov'd name!

No,— that hallow'd form is ne'er forgot,
  Which first love trac'd;
Still it lingering haunts the greenest spot
  On memory's waste.
  'Twas odor fled
  As soon as shed;
  'Twas morning's winged dream;
'Twas a light that ne'er can shine again
  On life's dull stream:
Oh! 'twas light that ne'er can shine again
  On life's dull stream.

THE PRINCE'S DAY.*

THO' dark are our sorrows, to-day we'll forget them,
    And smile through our tears, like a sunbeam in
        showers;
There never were hearts, if our rulers would let them,
    More form'd to be grateful and blest than ours.
        But just when the chain
        Has ceased to pain,
And hope has enwreath'd it round with flowers,
        There comes a new link
        Our spirits to sink —
O, the joy that we taste, like the light of the poles,
  Is a flash amid darkness, too brilliant to stay;
But though 'twere the last little spark in our souls,
  We must light it up now, on our Prince's Day.

Contempt on the minion, who calls you disloyal!
    Tho' fierce to your foe, to your friends you are true;
And the tribute most high to a head that is royal,
    Is love from a heart that loves liberty too.
        While cowards, who blight
        Your fame, your right,
Would shrink from the blaze of the battle array,
        The standard of Green
        In front would be seen —

* This song was written for a fête in honor of the Prince of Wales' birth day, given by my friend, Major Bryan, last year (1810) at his seat in the county of Kilkenny.

Oh, my life on your faith! were you summon'd this minute,
   You'd cast every bitter remembrance away,
And show what the arm of old Erin has in it,
   When rous'd by the foe on her Prince's Day.

He loves the Green Isle, and his love is recorded
   In hearts which have suffered too much to forget;
And hope shall be crown'd, and attachment rewarded,
   And Erin's gay jubilee shine out yet.
       The gem may be broke
       By many a stroke,
   But nothing can cloud its native ray;
       Each fragment will cast
       A light to the last,—
And thus Erin, my country, though broken thou art,
   There's a lustre within thee that ne'er will decay;
A spirit which beams through each suffering part,
   And now smiles at all pain on the Prince's Day.

WEEP ON, WEEP ON.

WEEP on, weep on, your hour is past;
   Your dreams of pride are o'er;
The fatal chain is round you cast,
   And you are men no more.
In vain the hero's heart hath bled;
   The sage's tongue hath warn'd in vain,—
Oh, Freedom! once thy flame hath fled,
   It never lights again!

Weep on — perhaps in after days
   They'll learn to love your name :
When many a deed may wake in praise
   That long hath slept in blame.
And when they tread the ruin'd aisle
   Where rest, at length, the lord and slave,
They'll wondering ask, how hands so vile
   Could conquer hearts so brave ?

" 'Twas fate," they'll say, " a wayward fate,
   Your web of discord wove ;
And while your tyrants join'd in hate,
   You never join'd in love.
But hearts fell off, that ought to twine,
   And man profan'd what God had given,
Till some were heard to curse the shrine,
   Where others knelt to heaven."

LESBIA HATH A BEAMING EYE.

LESBIA hath a beaming eye,
   But no one knows for whom it beameth;
Right and left its arrows fly,
   But what they aim at no one dreameth.
Sweeter 'tis to gaze upon
   My Nora's lid that seldom rises ;
Few its looks, but every one,
   Like unexpected light, surprises.
    Oh, my Nora Creina, dear,
   My gentle, bashful Nora Creina,

>   Beauty lies
>   In many eyes,
>   But love in yours, my Nora Creina!

Lesbia wears a robe of gold,
  But all so close the nymph hath laced it,
Not a charm of beauty's mould
  Presumes to stay where nature placed it.
O, my Nora's gown for me,
  That floats as wild as mountain breezes
Leaving every beauty free
  To sink or swell as Heaven pleases,
    Yes, my Nora Creina, dear,
My simple, graceful Nora Creina,
        Nature's dress
        Is loveliness —
The dress *you* wear, my Nora Creina.

Lesbia hath a wit refin'd,
  But when its points are gleaming round us,
Who can tell if they're design'd
  To dazzle merely, or to wound us?
Pillow'd on my Nora's heart
  In safer slumber Love reposes —
Bed of peace! whose roughest part
  Is but the crumpling of the roses.
    Oh, my Nora Creina dear,
My mild, my artless Nora Creina,
        Wit, though bright,
        Hath no such light
As warms your eyes, my Nora Creina.

I SAW THY FORM.

I SAW thy form in youthful prime,
  Nor thought that pale decay
Would steal before the steps of Time,
  And waste its bloom away, Mary!
Yet still thy features wore that light,
  Which fleet not with the breath;
And life ne'er look'd more truly bright
  Than in thy smile of death, Mary!

As streams that run o'er golden mines,
  Yet humbly, calmly glide,
Nor seem to know the wealth that shines
  Within their gentle tide, Mary!
So, veil'd beneath the simplest guise,
  Thy radiant genius shone,
And that which charm'd all other eyes,
  Seem'd worthless in thine own, Mary!

If souls could always dwell above,
  Thou ne'er hadst left that sphere;
Or could we keep the souls we love,
  We ne'er had lost thee here, Mary!
Though many a gifted mind we meet,
  Though fairest forms we see,
To live with them is far less sweet
  Than to remember thee, Mary!*

---

* I have here made a feeble effort to imitate that exquisite inscription of Shenstone's — "Heu! quanto minus est cum reliquis versari quam tui meminisse!"

BY THAT LAKE.*

BY that Lake, whose gloomy shore
    Skylark never warbles o'er, †
Where the cliff hangs high and steep,
Young Saint Kevin stole to sleep.
"Here, at least," he calmly said,
"Woman ne'er shall find my bed."
Ah! the good Saint little knew
What that wily sex can do.

'Twas from Kathleen's eyes he flew,
Eyes of most unholy blue!
She had lov'd him well and long,
Wish'd him hers, nor thought it wrong.
Wheresoe'er the Saint would fly,
Still he heard her light foot nigh;
East or west, where'er he turn'd,
Still her eyes before him burn'd.

On the bold cliff's bosom cast,
Tranquil now he sleeps at last;
Dreams of Heaven, nor thinks that e'er
Woman's smile can haunt him there.
But nor earth nor heaven is free
From her power, if fond she be:
Even now, while calm he sleeps,
Kathleen o'er him leans and weeps.

* This ballad is founded upon one of the many stories related of St Kevin, whose bed in the rock is to be seen at Glendalough, a most gloomy and romantic spot in the county of Wicklow.

† There are many other curious traditions concerning this lake, which may be found in Giraldus, Colgan, &c.

Fearless she had track'd his feet
To this rocky, wild retreat;
And, when morning met his view,
Her mild glances met it too.
Ah! your saints have cruel hearts!
Sternly from his bed he starts,
And with rude, repulsive shock,
Hurls her from the beetling rock.

Glendalough! thy gloomy wave
Soon was gentle Kathleen's grave!
Soon the Saint (yet ah! too late),
Felt her love, and mourn'd her fate.
When he said, "Heaven rest her soul!"
Round the Lake light music stole;
And her ghost was seen to glide,
Smiling, o'er the fatal tide!

SHE IS FAR FROM THE LAND.

SHE is far from the land where her young hero
    sleeps,
  And lovers are round her sighing;
But coldly she turns from their gaze, and weeps,
  For her heart in his grave is lying.

She sings the wild song of her dear native plains,
  Every note, which he lov'd, awaking;—
Ah! little they think, who delight in her strains,
  How the heart of the minstrel is breaking!

He had liv'd for his love, for his country he died,
    They were all that to life had entwin'd him;
Nor soon shall the tears of his country be dried,
    Nor long will his love stay behind him.

Oh! make her a grave where the sunbeams rest
    When they promise a glorious morrow;
They'll shine o'er her sleep, like a smile from the West,
    From her own lov'd island of sorrow.

NAY, TELL ME NOT.

NAY, tell me not, dear, that the goblet drowns
    One charm of feeling, one fond regret;
Believe me, a few of thy angry frowns
    Are all I've sunk in its bright wave yet.
        Ne'er hath a beam
        Been lost in the stream
That ever was shed from thy form or soul;
        The spell of those eyes,
        The balm of thy sighs,
Still float on the surface, and hallow my bowl.
Then fancy not, dearest, that wine can steal
    One blissful dream of the heart from me;
Like founts, that awaken the pilgrim's zeal,
    The bowl but brightens my love for thee.

They tell us that Love, in his fairy bower,
  Had two blush-roses of birth divine ;
He sprinkled the one with a rainbow's shower,
  But bath'd the other with mantling wine.
      Soon did the buds,
      That drank of the floods
Distill'd by the rainbow, decline and fade ;
      While those which the tide
      Of ruby had dy'd
All blush into beauty, like thee, sweet maid !
Then fancy not, dearest, that wine can steal
  One blissful dream of the heart from me ;
Like founts, that awaken the pilgrim's zeal,
  The bowl but brightens my love for thee !

AVENGING AND BRIGHT.*

AVENGING and bright fall the swift sword of Erin
  On him who the brave sons of Usna betray'd !—
For every fond eye he hath waken'd a tear in,
  A drop from his heart-wounds shall weep o'er her
    blade.

---

* The words of this song were suggested by the very ancient Irish story called 'Deirdri, or the Lamentable Fate of the Sons of Usnach,' which has been translated literally from the Gaelic by Mr O'Flanagan, (see vol. 1 of the Transactions of the Gaelic Society of Dublin), and upon which it appears that the 'Darthula' of Macpherson is founded. The treachery of Connor, king of Ulster, in putting to death the three sons of Usna, was the cause of a desolating war against Ulster, which terminated in the destruction of Eman. "This story," says Mr O'Flanagan, "has been from

By the red cloud that hung over Connor's dark dwel-
  ling,*
  When † Ulad's three champions lay sleeping in
    gore —
By the billows of war, which, so often high swelling,
  Have wafted these heroes to victory's shore —

We swear to revenge them!—no joy shall be tasted,
  The harp shall be silent, the maiden unwed,
Our halls shall be mute, and our fields shall lie wasted,
  Till vengeance is wreak'd on the murderer's head!

Yes, monarch! tho' sweet are our home recollections,
  Tho' sweet are the tears that from tenderness fall;
Though sweet are our friendships, our hopes, our
  affections,
  Revenge on a tyrant is sweetest of all!

---

time immemorial held in high repute, as one of the three tragic stories of the Irish. These are, ' The death of the children of Touran ;' ' The death of the children of Lear' (both regarding Tuatha de Danans) ; and this, ' The death of the children of Usnach,' which is a Milesian story." It will be recollected that, in another part of these Melodies, there is a ballad upon the story of the children of Lear or Lir ; ' Silent, O Moyle.'

Whatever may be thought of those sanguine claims to antiquity, which Mr O'Flanagan and others advance for the literature of Ireland, it would be a very lasting reproach upon our nationality, if the Gaelic researches of these gentlemen did not meet with all the liberal encouragement they merit.

* " O Nasi! view that cloud that I here see in the sky! I see over Eman-green a chilling cloud of blood-tinged red."—DEIRDRI'S Song.

† Ulster.

WHAT THE BEE IS.

He.—WHAT the bee is to the floweret,
    When he looks for honey dew,
Through the leaves that close embower it,
    That, my love, I'll be to you.

She.— What the bank, with verdure glowing,
    Is to waves that wander near,
Whispering kisses, while they're going,
    That I'll be to you, my dear.

She.— But, they say, the bee's a rover,
    Who will fly when sweets are gone;
And when once the kiss is over,
    Faithless brooks will wander on.

He.— Nay, if flowers *will* lose their looks,
    If sunny banks *will* wear away,
'Tis but right that bees and brooks
    Should sip and kiss them while they **may**.

LOVE AND THE NOVICE.

" HERE we dwell in holiest bowers,
    " Where angels of light o'er our orisons bend;
" Where sighs of devotion and breathings of flowers
    " To Heaven in mingled odor ascend.
    " Do not disturb our calm, O Love!
    " So like is thy form to the cherubs above,
" It well might deceive such hearts as ours."

Love stood near the Novice, and listen'd,
  And Love is no novice in taking a hint;
His laughing blue eyes soon with piety glisten'd;
  His rosy wing turn'd to heaven's own tint.
    "Who would have thought," the urchin cries,
    "That Love could so well, so gravely disguise
    "His wandering wings, and wounding eyes?"

Love now warms thee, waking or sleeping,
  Young Novice! to him all thy orisons rise;
He tinges the heavenly fount with his weeping,
  He brightens the censer's flame with his sighs.
    Love is the saint enshrined in thy breast,
    And angels themselves would admit such a guest,
    If he came to them cloth'd in Piety's vest.

THIS LIFE IS ALL CHEQUER'D.

THIS life is all chequer'd with pleasures and woes,
  That chase one another like waves of the deep;
Each brightly or darkly, as onward it flows,
  Reflecting our eyes, as they sparkle or weep.
So closely our whims on our miseries tread,
  That the laugh is awak'd ere the tear can be dried;
And, as fast as the rain-drop of Pity is shed,
  The goose-plumage of Folly can turn it aside.
But pledge me the cup — if existence would cloy,
  With hearts ever happy, and heads ever wise,
Be ours the light Sorrow, half-sister to Joy,
  And the light brilliant Folly that flashes and dies.

When Hylas was sent with his urn to the fount,
  Thro' fields full of light, with heart full of play,
Light rambled the boy over meadow and mount,
  And neglected his task for the flowers on the way.*
Thus many, like me, who in youth should have tasted
  The fountain that runs by Philosophy's shrine,
Their time with the flowers on the margin have wasted,
  And left their light urns all as empty as mine.
But pledge me the goblet — while Idleness weaves
  These flowerets together, should Wisdom but see
One bright drop or two that has fallen on the leaves
  From her fountain divine, 'tis sufficient for me.

OH THE SHAMROCK.

THROUGH Erin's Isle,
  To sport awhile,
As Love and Valor wander'd,
  With Wit the sprite,
  Whose quiver bright,
A thousand arrows squander'd;
  Where'er they pass,
  A triple grass †
Shoots up with dew-drops streaming,

---

* Proposito florem prætulit officio.
                          PROPERT. lib. i. eleg. 20.

† St Patrick is said to have made use of that species of the trefoil, to which in Ireland we give the name of Shamrock, in ex-

As softly green
As emeralds seen
Through purest crystal gleaming.
O the Shamrock! the green, immortal Shamrock!
Chosen leaf
Of bard and chief,
Old Erin's native Shamrock!

Says Valor, "See,
They spring for me,
Those leafy gems of morning!"
Says Love, "No, no,
For *me* they grow,
My fragrant path adorning."
But Wit perceives
The triple leaves,
And cries, "O do not sever
A type that blends
Three godlike friends,
Love, Valor, Wit, for ever!"
O the Shamrock! the green, immortal Shamrock!
Chosen leaf
Of bard and chief,
Old Erin's native Shamrock!

---

plaining the doctrine of the Trinity to the pagan Irish. I do not know if there be any other reason for our adoption of this plant as a national emblem. Hope, among the ancients, was sometimes represented as a beautiful child, standing on tiptoes, and a trefoil or three-colored grass in her hand.

So firmly fond
May last the bond
They wove that morn together,
And ne'er may fall
One drop of gall
On Wit's celestial feather!
May Love, as twine
His flowers divine,
Of thorny falsehood weed 'em!
May Valor ne'er
His standard rear
Against the cause of Freedom!
O the Shamrock! the green, immortal Shamrock!
Chosen leaf
Of bard and chief,
Old Erin's native Shamrock!

AT THE MID HOUR OF NIGHT.

AT the mid hour of night, when stars are weeping,
    I fly
To the lone vale we lov'd, when life shone warm in
    thine eye;
And I think oft, if spirits can steal from the regions
    of air,
To revisit past scenes of delight, thou wilt come to
    me there,
And tell me, our love is remember'd even in the sky!

Then I sing the wild song, 'twas once such pleasure
    to hear,
When our voices commingling, breath'd like one on
    the ear;
And as Echo far off through the vale my sad orison
    rolls,
I think, O my love! 'tis thy voice from the kingdom
    of Souls,*
Faintly answering still the notes that once were so
    dear.

ONE BUMPER AT PARTING.

ONE bumper at parting! — though many
  Have circled the board since we met,
The fullest, the saddest of any,
  Remains to be crown'd by us yet.
The sweetness that pleasure has in it
  Is always so slow to come forth,
That seldom, alas, till the minute
  It dies, do we know half its worth.
But come, — may our life's happy measure
  Be all of such moments made up;
They're born on the bosom of Pleasure,
  They die 'midst the tears of the cup.

---

* "There are countries," says Montaigne, "where they believe the souls of the happy live in all manner of liberty, in delightful fields; and that it is those souls repeating the words we utter, which we call Echo."

As onward we journey, how pleasant
　To pause and inhabit awhile
Those few sunny spots, like the present,
　That 'mid the dull wilderness smile!
But Time, like a pitiless master,
　Cries 'Onward!' and spurs the gay hours —
Ah! never doth time travel faster
　Than when his way lies among flowers.
But come — may our life's happy measure
　Be all of such moments made up;
They're born on the bosom of Pleasure,
　They die 'midst the tears of the cup.

We saw how the sun look'd in sinking,
　The waters beneath him how bright;
And now let our farewell of drinking
　Resemble that farewell of light.
You saw how he finish'd, by darting
　His beam o'er a deep billow's brim —
So, fill up, let's shine at our parting,
　In full liquid glory, like him.
And O, may our life's happy measure
　Of moments like this be made up;
'Twas born on the bosom of Pleasure,
　It dies 'mid the tears of the cup.

THE LAST ROSE OF SUMMER.

'TIS the last rose of summer
    Left blooming alone;
All her lovely companions
    Are faded and gone;
No flower of her kindred,
    No rose-bud is nigh
To reflect back her blushes,
    Or give sigh for sigh.

I'll not leave thee, thou lone one,
    To pine on the stem;
Since the lovely are sleeping,
    Go, sleep thou with them.
Thus kindly I scatter
    Thy leaves o'er the bed,
Where thy mates of the garden
    Lie scentless and dead.

So soon may *I* follow,
    When friendships decay,
And from Love's shining circle
    The gems drop away!
When true hearts lie wither'd,
    And fond ones are flown,
Oh! who would inhabit
    This bleak world alone?

THE YOUNG MAY MOON.

THE young May moon is beaming, love,
    The glow-worm's lamp is gleaming, love,
        How sweet to rove
        Through Morna's grove, *
When the drowsy world is dreaming, love!
Then awake! the heavens look bright, my dear,
'Tis never too late for delight, my dear,
        And the best of all ways
        To lengthen our days,
Is to steal a few hours from the night, my dear.

Now all the world is sleeping, love,
But the Sage his star-watch keeping, love,
        And I, whose star,
        More glorious far,
Is the eye from that casement peeping, love.
Then awake! — till rise of sun, my dear,
The Sage's glass we'll shun, my dear,
        Or, in watching the flight
        Of bodies of light,
He might happen to take thee for one, my dear!

---

*   "Steals silently to Morna's grove."

See a translation from the Irish, in Mr. Bunting's collection, by John Brown, one of my earliest college companions and friends; whose death was as singularly melancholy and unfortunate as his life had been amiable, honorable and exemplary.

THE MINSTREL BOY.

THE Minstrel-boy to the war is gone,
   In the ranks of death you'll find him;
His father's sword he has girded on,
   And his wild harp slung behind him.—
" Land of song!" said the warrior-bard,
   " Though all the world betrays thee,
" *One* sword, at least, thy rights shall guard,
   " *One* faithful harp shall praise thee!"

The Minstrel fell! — but the foeman's chain
   Could not bring his proud soul under;
The harp he lov'd ne'er spoke again,
   For he tore its chords asunder;
And said, " No chains shall sully thee,
   " Thou soul of love and bravery!
" Thy songs were made for the pure and free,
   " They shall never sound in slavery!"

THE SONG OF O'RUARK,

PRINCE OF BREFFNI.*

THE valley lay smiling before me,
   Where lately I left her behind;
Yet I trembled, and something hung o'er me,
   That sadden'd the joy of my mind.
I look'd for the lamp which, she told me,
   Should shine when her Pilgrim return'd;
But though darkness began to enfold me,
   No lamp from the battlements burn'd.

---

* These stanzas are founded upon an event of most melancholy importance to Ireland; if, as we are told by our Irish historians, it gave England the first opportunity of profiting by our divisions, and subduing us. The following are the circumstances, as related by O'Halloran. "The king of Leinster had long conceived a violent affection for Dearbhorgil, daughter to the king of Meath; and though she had been for some time married to O'Ruark, prince of Breffni, yet it could not restrain his passion. They carried on a private correspondence, and she informed him that O'Ruark intended soon to go on a pilgrimage, (an act of piety frequent in those days), and conjured him to embrace that opportunity of conveying her from a husband she detested to a lover she adored. Mac Murchad too punctually obeyed the summons, and had the lady conveyed to his capital of Ferns."—The monarch Roderick espoused the cause of O'Ruark, while Mac Murchad fled to England, and obtained the assistance of Henry II. "Such," adds Giraldus Cambrensis, "is the variable and fickle nature of woman, by whom all mischiefs in the world (for the most part) do happen and come, as may appear by Marcus Antoniũs, and by the destruction of Troy."

I flew to her chamber — 't was lonely,
  As if the lov'd tenant lay dead ; —
Ah ! would it were death, and death only !
  But no, the young false one had fled.
And there hung the lute, that could soften
  My very worst pains into bliss,
While the hand that had wak'd it so often
  Now throbb'd to a proud rival's kiss.

There *was* a time, falsest of women !
  When Breffni's good sword would have sought
That man, through a million of foemen,
  Who dar'd but to wrong thee *in thought !*
While now — O degenerate daughter
  Of Erin, how fallen is thy fame !
And through ages of bondage and slaughter,
  Our country shall bleed for thy shame.

Already the curse is upon her,
  And strangers her valleys profane ;
They come to divide — to dishonor,
  And tyrants they long will remain.
But, onward ! — the green banner rearing,
  Go, flesh every sword to the hilt ;
On *our* side is Virtue and Erin,
  On *theirs* is the Saxon and Guilt.

O HAD WE SOME BRIGHT LITTLE ISLE.

OH had we some bright little isle of our own,
In a blue summer ocean, far off and alone,
Where a leaf never dies in the still blooming bowers,
And the bee banquets on through a whole year of flowers;
    Where the sun loves to pause
      With so fond a delay,
    That the night only draws
      A thin veil o'er the day;
Where simply to feel that we breathe, that we live,
Is worth the best joy that life elsewhere can give.

There, with souls ever ardent and pure as the clime,
We should love as they lov'd in the first golden time;
The glow of the sunshine, the balm of the air,
Would steal to our hearts, and make all summer there.
    Wtth affection as free
      From decline as the bowers;
    And with hope, like the bee,
      Living always on flowers,
Our life should resemble a long day of light,
And our death come on holy and calm as the night.

FAREWELL.

FAREWELL! — but whenever you welcome the hour
That awakens the night-song of mirth in your bower,
Then think of the friend who once welcom'd it too,
And forgot his own griefs to be happy with you.
His griefs may return, not a hope may remain
Of the few that have brighten'd his pathway of pain,
But he ne'er will forget the short vision that threw
Its enchantments around him while lingering with you.

And still on that evening, when pleasure fills up
To the highest top sparkle each heart and each cup,
Where'er my path lies, be it gloomy or bright,
My soul, happy friends, shall be with you that night;
Shall join in your revels, your sports, and your wiles,
And return to me beaming all o'er with your smiles;
Too blest, if it tells me, that, 'mid the gay cheer,
Some kind voice had murmur'd, "I wish he were here!"

Let Fate do her worst, there are relics of joy,
Bright dreams of the past, which she cannot destroy;
And which come in the night-time of sorrow and care,
And bring back the features that joy us'd to wear.
Long, long be my heart with such memories fill'd!
Like the vase, in which roses have once been distill'd,
You may break, you may shatter the vase, if you will,
But the scent of the roses will hang round it still.

OH DOUBT ME NOT.

OH doubt me not! — the season
    Is o'er, when Folly made me rove,
And now the vestal, Reason,
    Shall watch the fire awak'd by Love.
Although this heart was early blown,
    And fairest hands disturb'd the tree,
They only shook some blossoms down,
    Its fruit has all been kept for thee.
    Then doubt me not — the season
        Is o'er, when Folly made me rove;
    And now the vestal, Reason,
        Shall watch the fire awak'd by love.

And though my lute no longer
    May sing of Passion's ardent spell,
Yet, trust me, all the stronger
    I feel the bliss I do not tell.
The bee through many a garden roves,
    And hums his lay of courtship o'er,
But when he finds the flower he loves,
    He settles there, and hums no more.
    Then doubt me not — the season
        Is o'er, when Folly kept me free;
    And now the vestal, Reason,
        Shall guard the flame awak'd by thee.

YOU REMEMBER ELLEN.*

YOU remember Ellen, our hamlet's pride,
   How meekly she bless'd her humble lot
When the stranger, William, had made her his bride,
   And love was the light of their lowly cot?
Together they toil'd through winds and rains,
   Till William at length in sadness said,
"We must seek our fortune on other plains;"—
   Then, sighing, she left her lowly shed.

They roam'd a long and a weary way,
   Nor much was the maiden's heart at ease,
When now, at close of one stormy day,
   They see a proud castle among the trees.
"To-night," said the youth, "we'll shelter there;
   "The wind blows cold, the hour is late;"
So he blew the horn with a chieftain's air,
   And the Porter bow'd as he pass'd the gate.

"Now welcome, Lady!" exclaimed the youth,
   "This castle is thine, and these dark woods all!"
She believ'd him craz'd, but his words were truth,
   For Ellen is Lady of Rosna Hall.
And dearly the Lord of Rosna loves
   What William the stranger woo'd and wed;
And the light of bliss, in these lordly groves,
   Shines pure as it did in the lowly shed.

* This ballad was suggested by a well-known and interesting story told of a certain noble family in England.

I'D MOURN THE HOPES.

I'D mourn the hopes that leave me,
  If thy smiles had left me too;
I'd weep when friends deceive me,
  If thou wert, like them, untrue.
But while I've thee before me,
  With heart so warm and eyes so bright,
No clouds can linger o'er me,
  That smile turns them all to light.

'Tis not in Fate to harm me,
  While Fate leaves thy love to me;
'Tis not in Joy to charm me,
  Unless Joy be shar'd with thee.
One minute's dream about thee
  Were worth a long, an endless year
Of waking bliss without thee,
  My own love, my only dear!

And though the hope be gone, love,
  That long sparkled o'er our way,
O, we shall journey on, love,
  More safely, without its ray.
Far better lights shall win me
  Along the path I've yet to roam:—
The mind that burns within me,
  And pure smiles from thee at home.

Thus, when the lamp that lighted
   The traveller at first goes out,
He feels awhile benighted,
   And looks round in fear and doubt.
But soon, the prospect clearing,
   By cloudless starlight on he treads,
And thinks no lamp so cheering
   As that light which Heaven sheds!

COME O'ER THE SEA.

COME o'er the sea,
   Maiden, with me,
Mine through sunshine, storm and snows;
   Seasons may roll,
   But the true soul
Burns the same, where'er it goes.
Let Fate frown on, so we love and part not;
'Tis life where *thou* art, 'tis death where thou art not.
   Then come o'er the sea,
   Maiden, with me,
Come wherever the wild wind blows;
   Seasons may roll,
   But the true soul
Burns the same, where'er it goes.

Was not the sea
Made for the Free,
Land for courts and chains alone?
   Here we are slaves,
   But on the waves
Love and Liberty's all our own.

No eye to watch, and no tongue to wound us,
All earth forgot, and all heaven around us —
    Then come o'er the sea,
    Maiden, with me,
Mine through sunshine, storm and snows;
    Seasons may roll,
    But the true soul
Burns the same, where'er it goes.

HAS SORROW THY YOUNG DAYS SHADED.

HAS sorrow thy young days shaded,
  As clouds o'er the morning fleet?
Too fast have those young days faded,
  That even in sorrow were sweet.
Does Time with his cold wing wither
  Each feeling that once was dear? —
Then, child of misfortune, come hither,
  I'll weep with thee tear for tear.

Has Love, to that soul so tender,
  Been like our Lagenian mine,*
Where sparkles of golden splendor
  All over the surface shine?
But if, in pursuit, we go deeper,
  Allured by the gleam that shone,
Ah! false as the dream of the sleeper,
  Like Love the bright ore is gone.

---

* Our Wicklow gold mines, to which this verse alludes, deserve, I fear, but too well the character here given of them.

Has Hope, like the bird in the story,*
    That flitted from tree to tree
With the talisman's glittering glory —
    Has Hope been that bird to thee?
On branch after branch alighting,
    The gem did she still display,
And, when nearest and most inviting,
    Then waft the fair gem away?

If thus the young hours have fleeted,
    When sorrow itself look'd bright;
If thus the fair hope hath cheated,
    That led thee along so light;
If thus the cold world now wither
    Each feeling that once was dear;—
Come, child of misfortune, come hither,
    I'll weep with thee tear for tear.

NO, NOT MORE WELCOME.

No, not more welcome the fairy numbers
    Of music fall on the sleeper's ear,
When, half awaking from fearful slumbers,
    He thinks the full quire of heaven is near,—

---

* " The bird, having got its prize, settled not far off, with the talisman in his mouth. The prince drew near it, hoping he would drop it : but, as he approached, the bird took wing, and settled again," &c.—ARABIAN NIGHTS, Story of Kummir al Zummaun.

Then came that voice, when, all forsaken,
    This heart long had sleeping lain,
Nor thought its cold pulse would ever waken
    To such benign, blessed sounds again.

Sweet voice of comfort! 'twas like the stealing
    Of summer wind thro' some wreathed shell—
Each secret winding, each inmost feeling
    Of my soul echo'd to its spell!
'Twas whisper'd balm — 'twas sunshine spoken!
    I'd live years of grief and pain
To have my long sleep of sorrow broken
    By such benign, blessed sounds again.

WHEN FIRST I MET THEE.

WHEN first I met thee, warm and young,
    There shone such truth about thee,
And on thy lip such promise hung,
    I did not dare to doubt thee.
I saw thee change, yet still relied,
    Still clung with hope the fonder,
And thought, though false to all beside,
    From me thou couldst not wander.
    But go, deceiver! go,—
        The heart, whose hopes could make it
    Trust one so false, so low,
        Deserves that thou shouldst break it.

When every tongue thy follies nam'd,
    I fled the unwelcome story;

Or found, in ev'n the faults they blam d,
  Some gleams of future glory.
I still was true, when nearer friends
  Conspir'd to wrong, to slight thee;
The heart that now thy falsehood rends,
  Would then have bled to right thee.
    But go, deceiver! go,—
      Some day perhaps thou'lt waken
    From pleasure's dream, to know
      The grief of hearts forsaken.

Ev'n now, though youth its bloom has shed,
  No lights of age adorn thee:
The few, who lov'd thee once, have fled,
  And they who flatter scorn thee.
Thy midnight cup is pledged to slaves,
  No genial ties enwreath it;
The smiling there, like light on graves,
  Has rank cold hearts beneath it.
    Go,— go,— though worlds were thine,
      I would not now surrender
    One taintless tear of mine
      For all thy guilty splendor!

And days may come, thou false one! yet,
  When even those ties shall sever;
When thou wilt call, with vain regret,
  On her thou'st lost forever,—
On her who, in thy fortune's fall,
  With smiles had still received thee,
And gladly died to prove thee all
  Her fancy first believed thee.

Go — go — 't is vain to curse,
  'Tis weakness to upbraid thee;
Hate cannot wish thee worse
  Than guilt and shame have made thee.

WHILE HISTORY'S MUSE.

WHILE History's Muse the memorial was keeping
  Of all that the dark hand of Destiny weaves,
Beside her the Genius of Erin stood weeping,
  For hers was the story that blotted the leaves.
But O, how the tear in her eyelids grew bright,
When, after whole pages of sorrow and shame,
    She saw History write
    With a pencil of light
That illum'd the whole volume, her Wellington's name!

"Hail, Star of my Isle!" said the Spirit, all sparkling
  With beams such as break from her own dewy skies —
"Through ages of sorrow, deserted and darkling,
  "I've watch'd for some glory like thine to arise.
"For though Heroes I've number'd, unblest was their lot,
"And unhallow'd they sleep in the cross-ways of Fame; —
    "But O there is not
    "One dishonoring blot
"On the wreath that encircles my Wellington's name!

" Yet still the last crown of thy toils is remaining,
" The grandest, the purest, e'en thou hast yet
known;
" Tho' proud was thy task, other nations unchaining,
" Far prouder to heal the deep wounds of thy own.
" At the foot of that throne for whose weal thou
hast stood,
" Go, plead for the land that first cradled thy fame—
" And bright o'er the flood
" Of her tears and her blood,
" Let the rainbow of hope be her Wellington's name!"

THE TIME I'VE LOST IN WOOING.

THE time I've lost in wooing,
    In watching and pursuing
        The light that lies
        In woman's eyes,
Has been my heart's undoing.
Though Wisdom oft has sought me,
I scorn'd the lore she brought me,
        My only books
        Were woman's looks,
And folly's all they've taught me.

Her smile when Beauty granted,
I hung with gaze enchanted,
        Like him the Sprite*
        Whom maids by night
Oft meet in glen that's haunted.

---

* This alludes to a kind of Irish fairy, which is to be met with, they say, in the fields at dusk;—as long as you keep your eyes

Like him, too, Beauty won me,
But while her eyes were on me,
    If once their ray
    Was turn'd away,
O, winds could not outrun me.

And are those follies going?
And is my proud heart growing
    Too cold or wise
    For brilliant eyes
Again to set it glowing?
No, — vain, alas, the endeavor
From bonds so sweet to sever; —
    Poor Wisdom's chance
    Against a glance
Is now as weak as ever.

OH WHERE'S THE SLAVE.

OH, where's the slave so lowly,
    Condemn'd to chains unholy,
        Who, could he burst
        His bonds at first,
Would pine beneath them slowly?

upon him, he is fixed, and in your power; but the moment you look away (and he is ingenious in furnishing some inducement) he vanishes. I had thought that this was the sprite which we call the Leprechaun; but a high authority upon such subjects, Lady Morgan (in a note upon her national and interesting novel, O'Donnel) has given a very different account of that goblin.

What soul, whose wrongs degrade it,
Would wait till time decay'd it,
  When thus its wing
  At once may spring
To the throne of Him who made it?

  Farewell, Erin,— farewell, all
  Who live to weep our fall!

Less dear the laurel growing,
Alive, untouch'd, and blowing,
  Than that whose braid
  Is pluck'd to shade
The brows with victory glowing.
We tread the land that bore us,
Her green flag glitters o'er us,
  The friends we've tried
  Are by our side,
And the foe we hate before us.

  Farewell, Erin,— farewell, all
  Who live to weep our fall!

COME, REST IN THIS BOSOM.

COME, rest in this bosom, my own stricken deer,
  Though the herd has fled from thee, thy home is still here;
Here still is the smile that no cloud can o'ercast,
And a heart and a hand all thy own to the last.

Oh, what was love made for, if 'tis not the same
Thro' joy and thro' torment, thro' glory and shame?
I know not, I ask not, if guilt's in that heart,
I but know that I love thee, whatever thou art.

Thou hast call'd me thy Angel, in moments of bliss,
And thy Angel I'll be, 'mid the horrors of this,—
Thro' the furnace, unshrinking, thy steps to pursue,
And shield thee, and save thee, or perish there too!

'TIS GONE AND FOREVER.

'TIS gone, and forever, the light we saw breaking,
   Like Heaven's first dawn o'er the sleep of the dead,
When Man, from the slumber of ages awaking,
   Look'd upward, and blest the pure ray, ere it fled.
'Tis gone, and the gleams it has left of its burning
But deepen the long night of bondage and mourning,
That dark o'er the kingdoms of earth is returning,
   And darkest of all, hapless Erin! o'er thee.

For high was thy hope, when those glories were darting
   Around thee, thro' all the gross clouds of the world;
When Truth, from her fetters indignantly starting,
   At once, like a Sun-burst, her banner unfurl'd.*
Oh, never shall earth see a moment so splendid!
Then, then,—had one Hymn of Deliverance blended
The tongues of all nations—how sweet had ascended
   The first note of Liberty, Erin, from thee!

* "The sun-burst" was the fanciful name given by the ancient Irish to the royal banner.

But, shame on those tyrants who envied the blessing !
　And shame on the light race unworthy its good,
Who, at Death's reeking altar, like furies caressing
　The young hope of Freedom, baptis'd it in blood !
Then vanish'd forever that fair, sunny vision,
Which, spite of the slavish, the cold heart's derision,
Shall long be remember'd, pure, bright, and elysian,
　As first it arose, my lost Erin ! on thee.

I SAW FROM THE BEACH.

I SAW from the beach, when the morning was shining,
　A bark o'er the waters move gloriously on ;
I came when the sun o'er that beach was declining,
　The bark was still there, but the waters were gone.

And such is the fate of our life's early promise,
　So passing the spring-tide of joy we have known ;
Each wave, that we danced on at morning, ebbs from us,
And leaves us, at eve, on the bleak shore alone.

Ne'er tell me of glories serenely adorning
　The close of day, the calm eve of our night ;
Give me back, give me back, the wild freshness of Morning,
　Her clouds and her tears are worth Evening's best light.

Oh, who would not welcome that moment's returning,
  When passion first wak'd a new life thro' his frame,
And his soul — like the wood that grows precious in
    burning —
  Gave out all its sweets to love's exquisite flame!

FILL THE BUMPER FAIR.

FILL the bumper fair!
    Every drop we sprinkle
O'er the brow of Care
    Smooths away a wrinkle.
Wit's electric flame
    Ne'er so swiftly passes,
As when through the frame
    It shoots from brimming glasses.
Fill the bumper fair!
    Every drop we sprinkle
O'er the brow of Care
    Smooths away a wrinkle.

Sages can, they say,
    Grasp the lightning's pinions,
And bring down its ray
    From the starr'd dominions;—
So we, Sages, sit
    And 'mid bumpers bright'ning,
From the heaven of Wit
    Draw down all its lightning.

Wouldst thou know what first
   Made our souls inherit
This ennobling thirst
   For wine's celestial spirit?
It chanced upon that day,
   When, as bards inform us,
Prometheus stole away
   The living fires that warm us.
The careless Youth, when up
   To Glory's fount aspiring,
Took nor urn nor cup
   To hide the pilfer'd fire in.—
But O his joy! when, round
   The halls of heaven spying,
Among the stars he found
   A bowl of Bacchus lying.

Some drops were in that bowl,
   Remains of last night's pleasure,
With which the Sparks of Soul
   Mix'd their burning treasure.
Hence the goblet's shower
   Hath such spells to win us;
Hence its mighty power
   O'er that flame within us.
Fill the bumper fair!
   Every drop we sprinkle
O'er the brow of Care
   Smooths away a wrinkle.

DEAR HARP OF MY COUNTRY.

DEAR Harp of my Country! in darkness I found thee,
    The cold chain of silence had hung o'er thee long,*
When proudly, my own Island Harp, I unbound thee,
    And gave all thy chords to light, freedom and song!
The warm lay of love, and the light note of gladness
    Have waken'd thy fondest, thy liveliest thrill;
But so oft hast thou echoed the deep sigh of sadness,
    That e'en in thy mirth it will steal from thee still.

Dear Harp of my Country! farewell to thy numbers,
    This sweet wreath of song is the last we shall twine!
Go, sleep with the sunshine of Fame on thy slumbers,
    Till touch'd by some hand less unworthy than mine.
If the pulse of the patriot, soldier, or lover,
    Have throbb'd at our lay, 'tis thy glory alone;
I was *but* as the wind, passing heedlessly over,
    And all the wild sweetness I wak'd was thy own.

---

* In that rebellious but beautiful song, "When Erin first rose," there is, if I recollect right, the following line —

'The dark chain of silence was thrown o'er the deep.'

The Chain of Silence was a sort of practical figure of rhetoric among the ancient Irish. Walker tells us of "a celebrated contention for precedence between Finn and Gaul, near Finn's palace at Almhaim, where the attending bards, anxious, if possible, to produce a cessation of hostilities, shook the Chain of Silence, and flung themselves among the ranks." See also the Ode to Gaul, in Miss Brookes's Reliques of Irish Poetry.

MY GENTLE HARP.

My gentle Harp! once more I waken
　The sweetness of thy slumbering strain;
In tears our last farewell was taken,
　And now in tears we meet again.
No light of joy hath o'er thee broken,
　But, like those Harps whose heavenly skill
Of slavery, dark as thine, hath spoken,
　Thou hang'st upon the willows still.

And yet, since last thy chord resounded,
　An hour of peace and triumph came,
And many an ardent bosom bounded
　With hopes — that now are turn'd to shame.
Yet even then, while peace was singing
　Her halcyon song o'er land and sea,
Though joy and hope to others bringing,
　She only brought new tears to thee.

Then, who can ask for notes of pleasure,
　My drooping Harp, from chords like thine?
Alas, the lark's gay morning measure
　As ill would suit the swan's decline!
Or how shall I, who love, who bless thee,
　Invoke thy breath for Freedom's strains,
When ev'n the wreaths in which I dress thee
　Are sadly mix'd — half flowers, half chains?

But come,— if yet thy frame can borrow
  One breath of joy, O breathe for me,
And show the world, in chains and sorrow,
  How sweet thy music still can be;
How gaily, ev'n 'mid gloom surrounding
  Thou yet canst wake at pleasure's thrill —
Like Memnon's broken image sounding,
  'Mid desolation, tuneful still.*

AS SLOW OUR SHIP.

AS slow our ship her foamy track
  Against the wind was cleaving,
Her trembling pennant still look'd back
  To that dear isle 'twas leaving :—
So loath we part from all we love,
  From all the links that bind us;
So turn our hearts, as on we rove,
  To those we've left behind us.

When, round the bowl, of vanish'd years
  We talk, with joyous seeming,—
With smiles that might as well be tears,
  So faint, so sad, their beaming;
While memory brings us back again
  Each early tie that twin'd us,
Oh, sweet's the cup that circles then
  To those we've left behind us!

---

* "Dimidio magicæ resonant ubi Memnone chordæ." JUVENAL.

And when, in other climes, we meet
   Some isle, or vale enchanting,
Where all looks flowery, wild, and sweet,
   And nought but love is wanting;
We think how great had been our bliss
   If Heaven had but assign'd us
To live and die in scenes like this,
   With some we've left behind us!

As travellers oft look back at eve,
   When eastward darkly going,
To gaze upon that light they leave
   Still faint behind them glowing,—
So, when the close of pleasure's day
   To gloom hath near consign'd us,
We turn to catch one fading ray
   Of joy that's left behind us.

IN THE MORNING OF LIFE.

In the morning of life, when its cares are unknown,
   And its pleasures in all their new lustre begin,
When we live in a bright beaming world of our own,
   And the light that surrounds us is all from within;
Oh 'tis not, believe me, in that happy time
   We can love, as in hours of less transport we may;
Of our smiles, of our hopes, 'tis the gay sunny prime,
   But affection is truest when these fade away.

When we see the first glory of youth pass us by,
  Like a leaf on the stream that will never return;
When our cup, which had sparkled with pleasure so
    high,
  First tastes of the *other*, the dark-flowing urn;
Then, then is the time when affection holds sway
  With a depth and a tenderness joy never knew;
Love, nurs'd among pleasures, is faithless as they,
  But the Love born of Sorrow, like sorrow, is true.

In climes full of sunshine, tho' splendid the flowers,
  Their sighs have no freshness, their odor no worth;
'Tis the cloud and the mist of our own Isle of showers
  That call the rich spirit of fragrancy forth.
So it is not 'mid splendor, prosperity, mirth,
  That the depth of Love's generous spirit appears;
To the sunshine of smiles it may first owe its birth,
  But the soul of its sweetness is drawn out by tears.

WHEN COLD IN THE EARTH.

WHEN cold in the earth lies the friend thou hast
    lov'd,
  Be his faults and his follies forgot by thee then;
Or, if from their slumber the veil be remov'd,
  Weep o'er them in silence, and close it again.
And O, if 'tis pain to remember how far
  From the pathways of light he was tempted to
    roam,
Be it bliss to remember that thou wert the star
  That arose on his darkness, and guided him home.

From thee and thy innocent beauty first came
　The revealings that taught him true love to adore,
To feel the bright presence, and turn him with shame
　From the idols he blindly had knelt to before.
O'er the waves of a life long benighted and wild,
　Thou cam'st like a soft golden calm o'er the sea;
And if happiness purely and glowingly smiled
　On his evening horizon, the light was from thee.

And tho', sometimes, the shades of past folly might rise,
　And tho' falsehood again would allure him to stray,
He but turn'd to the glory that dwelt in those eyes,
　And the folly, the falsehood, soon vanish'd away.
As the Priests of the Sun, when their altar grew dim,
　At the day-beam alone could its lustre repair,
So, if virtue a moment grew languid in him,
　He but flew to that smile, and rekindled it there.

REMEMBER THEE.

REMEMBER thee? yes, while there's life in this heart
It shall never forget thee, all lorn as thou art;
More dear in thy sorrow, thy gloom, and thy showers,
Than the rest of the world in their sunniest hours.

Wert thou all that I wish thee, great, glorious, and free,
First flower of the earth, and first gem of the sea,

I might hail thee with prouder, with happier brow,
But O, could I love thee more deeply than now?

No, thy chains as they rankle, thy blood as it runs,
But make thee more painfully dear to thy sons —
Whose hearts, like the young of the desert-bird's nest,
Drink love in each life drop that flows from thy
    breast.

WREATH THE BOWL.

WREATH the bowl
    With flowers of soul,
The brightest Wit can find us;
    We'll take a flight
    Towards heaven to-night,
And leave dull earth behind us.
    Should Love amid
    The wreaths be hid,
That Joy, the enchanter, brings us,
    No danger fear,
    While wine is near,
We'll drown him if he stings us.

    Then wreath the bowl
    With flowers of soul,
The brightest Wit can find us;
    We'll take a flight
    Towards heaven to-night,
And leave dull earth behind us.

'T was nectar fed
Of old, 'tis said,
Their Junos, Joves, Apollos;
And man may brew
His nectar too,
The rich receipt 's as follows:
Take wine like this,
Let looks of bliss
Around it well be blended,
Then bring Wit's beam
To warm the stream,
And there's your nectar splendid!
So, wreath the bowl
With flowers of soul,
The brightest Wit can find us;
We'll take a flight
Towards heaven to-night,
And leave dull earth behind us.

Say, why did Time
His glass sublime
Fill up with sands unsightly,
When wine, he knew,
Runs brisker through,
And sparkles far more brightly?
Oh, lend it us,
And smiling thus,
The glass in two we'll sever,
Make pleasure glide
In double tide,
And fill both ends for ever!

Then wreath the bowl
With flowers of soul,
The brightest Wit can find us;
We'll take a flight
Towards heaven to-night,
And leave dull earth behind us.

WHENE'ER I SEE THOSE SMILING EYES.

WHENE'ER I see those smiling eyes,
  So full of hope, and joy, and light,
As if no cloud could ever rise,
  To dim a heaven so purely bright —
I sigh to think how soon that brow
  In grief may lose its every ray,
And that light heart, so joyous now,
  Almost forget it once was gay.

For time will come with all its blights,
  The ruin'd hope, the friend unkind,
And love, that leaves where'er it lights
  A chill'd or burning heart behind;—
While youth, that now like snow appears,
  Ere sullied by the darkening rain,
When once 'tis touch'd by sorrow's tears
  Will never shine so bright again.

IF THOU'LT BE MINE.

IF thou'lt be mine, the treasures of air,
  Of earth, and sea, shall lie at thy feet;
Whatever in Fancy's eye looks fair,
  Or in Hope's sweet music sounds *most* sweet,
    Shall be ours—if thou wilt be mine, love!

Bright flowers shall bloom wherever we rove,
  A voice divine shall talk in each stream,
The stars shall look like worlds of love,
  And this earth be all one beautiful dream
    In our eyes — if thou wilt be mine, love!

And thoughts whose source is hidden and high,
  Like streams that come from heavenward hills,
Shall keep our hearts, like meads that lie
  To be bath'd by those eternal rills,
    Ever green, if thou wilt be mine, love!

All this and more the Spirit of Love
  Can breathe o'er them who feel his spells;
That heaven, which forms his home above,
  He can make on earth, wherever he dwells,
    As thou'lt own, if thou wilt be mine, love!

TO LADIES' EYES.

TO Ladies' eyes around, boy,
  We can't refuse, we can't refuse,
Though bright eyes so abound, boy,
  'Tis hard to choose, 'tis hard to choose.
For thick as stars that lighten
  Yon airy bowers, yon airy bowers,
The countless eyes that brighten
  This earth of ours, this earth of ours.
But fill the cup — where'er, boy,
  Our choice may fall, our choice may fall,
We're sure to find Love there, boy,
  So drink them all! so drink them all!

Some looks there are so holy,
  They seem but given, they seem but given,
As shining beacons, solely,
  To light to heaven, to light to heaven.
While some — O, ne'er believe them! —
  With tempting ray, with tempting ray,
Would lead us (God forgive them!)
  The other way, the other way.
But fill the cup — where'er, boy,
  Our choice may fall, our choice may fall,
We're sure to find Love there, boy,
  So drink them all! so drink them all!

In some, as in a mirror,
  Love seems portray'd, Love seems portray'd,
But shun the flattering error,
  'Tis but his shade, 'tis but his shade.

Himself has fixed his dwelling
　　In eyes we know, in eyes we know,
And lips — but this is telling —
　　So here they go! so here they go!
Fill up, fill up — where'er, boy,
　　Our choice may fall, our choice may fall,
We're sure to find Love there, boy,
　　So drink them all! so drink them all!

FORGET NOT THE FIELD.

FORGET not the field where they perish'd,
　　The truest, the last of the brave,
All gone — and the bright hopes we cherish'd
　　Gone with them, and quench'd in their grave!

Oh! could we from death but recover
　　Those hearts as they bounded before,
In the face of high Heaven to fight over
　　That combat for freedom once more ;—

Could the chain for an instant be riven
　　Which tyranny flung round us then,
No! 'tis not in Man, nor in Heaven,
　　To let Tyranny bind it again!

But 'tis past — and though blazon'd in story
　　The name of our Victor may be,
Accurst is the march of that glory
　　Which treads o'er the hearts of the free.

Far dearer the grave or the prison
  Illum'd by one patriot name,
Than the trophies of all who have risen
  On Liberty's ruins to fame.

THEY MAY RAIL AT THIS LIFE.

THEY may rail at this life — from the hour I began it,
  I found it a life full of kindness and bliss;
And until they can show me some happier planet,
  More social and bright, I'll content me with this.
As long as the world has such lips and such eyes,
  As before me this moment enraptur'd I see,
They may say what they will of their orbs in the skies,
  But this earth is the planet for you, love, and me.

In Mercury's star, where each moment can bring them
  New sunshine and wit from the fountain on high,
Though the nymphs may have livelier poets to sing them,*
  They've none, even there, more enamor'd than I.
And, as long as this harp can be waken'd to love,
  And that eye its divine inspiration shall be,
They may talk as they will of their Edens above,
  But this earth is the planet for you, love, and me.

* "Tous les habitans de Mercure sont vifs."—PLURALITE DES MONDES.

In that star of the west, by whose shadowy splendor
   At twilight so often we've roam'd thro' the dew,
There are maidens, perhaps, who have bosoms as tender,
   And look, in their twilights, as lovely as you.*
But tho' they were even more bright than the queen
   Of that isle they inhabit in heaven's blue sea,
As I never those fair young celestials have seen,
   Why—this earth is the planet for you, love, and me.

As for those chilly orbs on the verge of creation,
   Where sunshine and smiles must be equally rare,
Did they want a supply of cold hearts for that station,
   Heaven knows we have plenty on earth we could spare.
O think what a world we should have of it here,
   If the haters of peace, of affection, and glee,
Were to fly up to Saturn's comfortless sphere,
   And leave earth to such spirits as you, love, and me.

OH FOR THE SWORDS.

OH for the swords of former time!
   Oh for the men who bore them.
When, arm'd for Right, they stood sublime,
   And tyrants crouch'd before them!

---

* 'La Terre pourra être pour Vénus l'etoile du berger et le mère des amours, comme Vénus l'est pour nos.'—PLUR. DES MONDES.

When free yet, ere courts began
  With honors to enslave him,
The best honors worn by Man
  Were those which Virtue gave him.
Oh for the swords, &c.

Oh for the kings who flourished then!
  Oh for the pomp that crown'd them,
When hearts and hands of freeborn men
  Were all the ramparts round them!
When, safe built on bosoms true,
  The throne was but the centre,
Round which Love a circle drew,
  That Treason durst not enter.
Oh for the Kings who flourished then!
  Oh for the pomp that crown'd them,
When hearts and hands of freeborn men
  Were all the ramparts round them!

NE'ER ASK THE HOUR.

NE'ER ask the hour—what is it to us
  How Time deals out his treasures?
The golden moments lent us thus
  Are not *his* coin, but Pleasure's.
If counting them o'er could add to their blisses,
  I'd number each glorious second;
But moments of joy are, like Lesbia's kisses,
  Too quick and sweet to be reckon'd.

Then fill the cup—what is it to us
  How Time his circle measures?
The fairy hours we call up thus
  Obey no wand but Pleasure's.

Young Joy ne'er thought of counting hours,
  Till Care, one summer's morning,
Set up, among his smiling flowers,
  A dial, by way of warning.
But Joy lov'd better to gaze on the sun,
  As long as its light was glowing,
Than to watch with old Care how the shadow stole on,
  And how fast that light was going.

  So fill the cup—what is it to us
    How Time his circle measures?
  The fairy hours we call up thus
    Obey no wand but Pleasure's.

SAIL ON, SAIL ON.

SAIL on, sail on, thou fearless bark —
  Wherever blows the welcome wind,
It cannot lead to scenes more dark,
  More sad than those we leave behind.
Each wave that passes seems to say,
  " Though death beneath our smile may be,
" Less cold we are, less false than they,
  " Whose smiling wreck'd thy hopes and thee."

Sail on, sail on — through endless space —
  Thro' calm — thro' tempest — stop no more;
The stormiest sea's a resting place
  To him who leaves such hearts on shore.
Or — if some desert land we meet,
  Where never yet false-hearted men
Profan'd a world that else were sweet,—
  Then rest thee, bark, but not till then.

THE PARALLEL.

YES, sad one of Sion*— if closely resembling,
  In shame and in sorrow, thy wither'd-up heart—
If drinking deep, deep of the same 'cup of trembling'
  Could make us thy children, our parent thou art.

Like thee doth our nation lie conquer'd and broken,
  And fall'n from her head is the once royal crown;
In her streets, in her halls, Desolation has spoken,
  And while it is day yet, 'her sun hath gone down.'†

Like thine doth her exile, 'mid dreams of returning,
  Die far from the home it were life to behold;
Like thine do her sons, in the day of their mourning,
  Remember the bright things that blest them of old.

* These verses were written after the perusal of a treatise by Mr Hamilton, professing to prove that the Irish were once Jews.

† "Her sun is gone down while it was yet day."—JER. XV. 9.

Ah, well may we call her like thee, 'the Forsaken,'*
  Her boldest are vanquish'd, her proudest are slaves;
And the harps of her minstrels, when gayest they waken,
  Have tones mid their mirth like the wind over graves!

Yet hadst thou thy vengeance,— yet came there the morrow
  That shines out at last on the longest dark night,
When the sceptre that smote thee with slavery and sorrow,
  Was shivered at once, like a reed, in thy sight.

When that cup, which for others the proud Golden City†
  Had brimm'd full of bitterness, drenched her own lips;
And the world she had trampled on heard, without pity,
  The howl in her halls, and the cry from her ships.

When the curse Heaven keeps for the haughty came over
  Her merchants rapacious, her rulers unjust,
And, a ruin, at last, for the earth-worm to cover,‡
  The Lady of Kingdoms lay low in the dust.‖

---

* 'Thou shalt no more be termed Forsaken.'—Isa. lxii. 4.

† 'How hath the oppressor ceased! the golden city ceased!'—Isa. xiv. 4.

‡ 'Thy pomp is brought down to the grave, ... and the worms cover thee.'—Isa. xiv. 11.

‖ 'Thou shalt no more be called the Lady of Kingdoms.'—Isa. xlvii. 5.

DRINK OF THIS CUP.

DRINK of this cup — you'll find there's a spell in
  Its every drop 'gainst the ills of mortality —
Talk of the cordial that sparkled for Helen,
  Her cup was a fiction, but this is reality.
Would you forget the dark world we are in,
  Just taste of the bubble that gleams on the top of it;
But would you rise above earth, till akin
  To Immortals themselves, you must drain every
      drop of it.
Send round the cup — for O there's a spell in
  Its every drop 'gainst the ills of mortality —
Talk of the cordial that sparkled for Helen,
  Her cup was a fiction, but this is reality.

Never was philter form'd with such power
  To charm and bewilder as this we are quaffing;
Its magic began when, in Autumn's rich hour,
  A harvest of gold in the fields it stood laughing.
There having, by Nature's enchantment, been fill'd
  With the balm and the bloom of her kindliest weather,
This wonderful juice from its core was distilled,
  To enliven such hearts as are here brought together.
Then drink of the cup — you'll find there's a spell in
  Its every drop 'gainst the ills of mortality —
Talk of the cordial that sparkled for Helen,
  Her cup was a fiction, but this is reality.

And though, perhaps — but breathe it to no one —
　Like liquor the witch brews at midnight so awful,
This philter in secret was first taught to flow on,
　Yet 't is n't less potent for being unlawful.
And e'en though it taste of the smoke of that flame
　Which in silence extracted its virtue forbidden —
Fill up — there's a fire in some hearts I could name,
　Which may work too its charm, though as lawless and hidden.
So drink of the cup — for O, there's a spell in
　Its every drop 'gainst the ills of mortality —
Talk of the cordial that sparkled for Helen,
　Her cup was a fiction, but this is reality.

THE FORTUNE TELLER.

DOWN in the valley come meet me to-night,
　And I'll tell you your fortune truly
As ever 'twas told, by the new-moon's light,
　To a young maiden, shining as newly.

But, for the world, let no one be nigh,
　Lest haply the stars should deceive me;
Such secrets between you and me and the sky
　Should never go farther, believe me.

If at that hour the heavens be not dim,
　My science shall call up before you
A male apparition — the image of him
　Whose destiny 'tis to adore you.

And if to that phantom you'll be kind,
  So fondly around you he'll hover,
You'll hardly, my dear, any difference find
  'Twixt him and a true living lover.

Down at your feet, in the pale moonlight,
  He'll kneel, with a warmth of devotion —
An ardor, of which such an innocent sprite
  You'd scarcely believe had a notion.

What other thoughts and events may arise,
  As in destiny's book I've not seen them,
Must only be left to the stars and your eyes
  To settle, ere morning, between them.

OH, YE DEAD.

OH, ye Dead! O, ye Dead! whom we know by the light you give
From your cold gleaming eyes, though you move like men who live,
    Why leave you thus your graves,
    In far-off fields and waves,
Where the worm and the sea-bird only know your bed,
    To haunt this spot, where all
    Those eyes that wept your fall,
And the hearts that wail'd you, like your own, lie dead?

It is true, it is true, we are shadows cold and wan;
And the fair and the brave whom we lov'd on earth are gone;

But still, thus ev'n in death,
So sweet the living breath
Of the fields and the flowers in our youth we wander'd o'er,
That ere, condemn'd, we go
To freeze 'mid Hecla's snow,*
We would taste it awhile, and think we live once more !

O'DONOHUE'S MISTRESS.

OF all the fair months that round the sun
In light-link'd dance their circles run,
  Sweet May, shine thou for me ;
For still, when thy earliest beams arise,
That youth, who beneath the blue lake lies,
  Sweet May, returns to me.

Of all the bright haunts where daylight leaves
Its lingering smile on golden eves,
  Fair Lake, thou'rt dearest to me ;
For, when the last April sun grows dim,
Thy Naiads prepare his steed for him†
  Who dwells, bright Lake, in thee.

---

* Paul Zealand mentions that there is a mountain in some part of Ireland, where the ghosts of persons who have died in foreign lands walk about and converse with those they meet, like living people. If asked why they do not return to their homes, they say they are obliged to go to Mount Hecla, and disappear immediately.
† The particulars of the tradition respecting O'Donohue and his White Horse may be found in Mr Weld's Account of Killarney, or

Of all the proud steeds that ever bore
Young plumed Chiefs on sea or shore,
    White Steed, most joy to thee ;
Who still, with the first young glance of spring,
From under that glorious lake dost bring
    My love, my Chief, to me.

While, white as the sail some bark unfurls,
When newly launched, thy long mane curls,*
    Fair Steed, as white and free ;
And spirits, from all the lake's deep bowers,
Glide o'er the blue wave, scattering flowers
    Around my love and thee.

Of all the sweet deaths that maidens die,
Whose lovers beneath the cold wave lie,
    Most sweet that death will be,
Which, under the next May evening's light,
When thou and thy steed are lost to sight,
    Dear love, I'll die for thee.

more fully detailed in Derrick's Letters. For many years after his death, the spirit of this hero is supposed to have been seen on the morning of May-day, gliding over the lake on his favorite white horse, to the sound of sweet unearthly music, and preceded by groups of youths and maidens, who flung wreaths of delicate spring flowers in his path.

Among other stories connected with this Legend of the Lakes it is said that there was a young and beautiful girl, whose imagination was so impressed with the idea of this visionary chieftain, that she fancied herself in love with him, and at last, in a fit of insanity, on a May morning, threw herself into the lake.

* The boatmen at Killarney call those waves which come on a windy day, crested with foam, "O'Donohue's white horses."

ECHO.

How sweet the answer Echo makes
    To Music at night,
When, roused by lute or horn, she wakes,
And, far away, o'er lawns and lakes,
    Goes answering light!

Yet Love hath echoes truer far,
    And far more sweet,
Than e'er beneath the moonlight's star,
Of horn, or lute, or soft guitar,
    The songs repeat.

'Tis when the sigh, in youth sincere,
    And only then,—
The sigh that's breath'd for one to hear,
Is by that one, that only dear,
    Breath'd back again.

OH BANQUET NOT.

Oh banquet not in those shining bowers
  Where youth resorts — but come to me;
For mine's a garden of faded flowers,
  More fit for sorrow, for age, and thee.
And there we shall have our feast of tears,
  And many a cup in silence pour;
Our guests, the shades of former years,
  Our toasts to lips that bloom no more.

There, while the myrtle's withering boughs
   Their lifeless leaves around us shed,
We'll brim the bowl to broken vows,
   To friends long lost, the changed, the dead.
Or, while some blighted laurel waves
   Its branches o'er the dreary spot,
We'll drink to those neglected graves,
   Where valor sleeps, unnamed, forgot.

THEE, THEE, ONLY THEE.

THE dawning of morn, the daylight's sinking,
   The night's long hours still find me thinking
      Of thee, thee, only thee.
When friends are met, and goblets crown'd,
   And smiles are near that once enchanted,
Unreach'd by all that sunshine round,
   My soul, like some dark spot, is haunted
      By thee, thee, only thee.

Whatever in fame's high path could waken
My spirit once is now forsaken
      For thee, thee, only thee.
Like shores by which some headlong bark
   To the ocean hurries, resting never,
Life's scenes go by me, bright or dark
   I know not, heed not, hastening ever
      To thee, thee, only thee.

I have not a joy but of thy bringing,
And pain itself seems sweet when springing
 From thee, thee, only thee.
Like spells that naught on earth can break,
 Till lips that know the charm have spoken,
This heart, howe'er the world make wake
 Its grief, its scorn, can but be broken
  By thee, thee, only thee.

SHALL THE HARP THEN BE SILENT.

SHALL the Harp then be silent, when he who first gave
 To our country a name is withdrawn from all eyes?
Shall a Minstrel of Erin stand mute by the grave
 Where the first—where the last of her Patriots lies?

No—faint tho' the death-song may fall from his lips,
 Though his Harp, like his soul, may with shadows be crost,
Yet, yet shall it sound, 'mid a nation's eclipse,
 And proclaim to the world what a star hath been lost.*

What a union of all the affections and powers
 By which life is exalted, embellished, refined,
Was embraced in that spirit—whose centre was ours,
 While its mighty circumference circled mankind?

---

* It is only the first two verses that are either fitted or intended to be sung.

Oh, who that loves Erin, or who that can see,
  Thro' the waste of her annals, that epoch sublime —
Like a pyramid rais'd in the desert — where he
  And his glory stand out to the eyes of all time;

That *one* lucid interval, snatched from the gloom
  And the madness of ages, when fill'd with his soul,
A nation o'erleap'd the dark bounds of her doom,
  And for *one* sacred instant touch'd Liberty's goal—

Who, that ever hath heard him — hath drank at the source
  Of that wonderful eloquence, all Erin's own,
In whose high-thoughted daring, the fire, and the force,
  And the yet untam'd spring of her spirit are shown;

An eloquence rich, wheresoever its wave
  Wander'd free and triumphant, with thoughts that shone through,
As clear as the brook's 'stone of lustre,' that gave,
  With the flash of the gem, its solidity too —

Who, that ever approached him, when free from the crowd,
  In a home full of love, he delighted to tread
'Mong the trees which a nation had giv'n, and which bow'd,
  As if each brought a new civic crown for his head—

Is there one who hath thus, through his orbit of life,
  But at distance observ'd him — through glory, through blame,
In the calm of retreat, in the grandeur of strife,
  Whether shining or clouded, still high and the same —

Oh no, not a heart that e'er knew him but mourns
  Deep, deep o'er the grave where such glory is shrin'd —
O'er a monument Fame will preserve 'mong the urns
  Of the wisest, the bravest, the best of mankind.

———

OH THE SIGHT ENTRANCING.

Oh, the sight entrancing,
When morning beam is glancing
    O'er files array'd
    With helm and blade,
And plumes in the gay wind dancing!
When hearts are all high beating,
And the trumpet's voice repeating
    That song whose breath
    May lead to death,
But never to retreating.
  Oh, the sight entrancing,
    When morning's beam is glancing

O'er files array'd
  With helm and blade,
And plumes in the gay wind dancing.

Yet, 't is not helm or feather —
For ask yon despot, whether
    His plumed bands
    Could bring such hands
And hearts as ours together.
Leave pomps to those who need 'em —
Give man but heart and freedom,
    And proud he braves
    The gaudiest slaves
That crawl where monarchs lead 'em.
The sword may pierce the beaver,
Stone walls in time may sever,
    'T is mind alone,
    Worth steel and stone,
That keeps men free for ever.
Oh that sight entrancing.
When the morning beam is glancing
    O'er files array'd
    With helm and blade,
And in Freedom's cause advancing!

SWEET INNISFALLEN.

SWEET Innisfallen, fare thee well,
  May calm and sunshine long be thine!
How fair thou art let others tell,
  To *feel* how fair shall long be mine.

Sweet Innisfallen, long shall dwell
  In memory's dream that sunny smile
Which o'er thee on that evening fell,
  When first I saw thy fairy isle.

'T was light, indeed, too blest for one
  Who had to turn to paths of care —
Through crowded haunts again to run,
  And leave thee bright and silent there:

No more unto thy shores to come,
  But, on the world's rude ocean tost,
Dream of thee sometimes, as a home
  Of sunshine he had seen and lost.

Far better in thy weeping hours
  To part from thee, as I do now,
When mist is o'er thy blooming bowers,
  Like sorrow's veil on beauty's brow.

For, though unrivall'd still thy grace,
  Thou dost not look, as then, *too* blest,
But, thus in shadow, seem'st a place
  Where erring man might hope to rest —

Might hope to rest, and find in thee
   A gloom like Eden's on the day
He left its shade, when every tree,
   Like thine, hung weeping o'er his way.

Weeping or smiling, lovely isle !
   And all the lovelier for thy tears —
For, though but rare thy sunny smile,
   'T is heav'n's own glance when it appears.

Like feeling hearts, whose joys are few
   But, when *indeed* they come, divine —
The brightest light the sun e'er threw
   Is lifeless to one gleam of thine.

'T WAS ONE OF THOSE DREAMS.*

'TWAS one of those dreams that by music are brought,
Like a bright summer haze, o'er the poet's warm thought —
When, lost in the future, his soul wanders on,
And all of this life, but its sweetness, is gone.

The wild notes he heard o'er the water were those
He had taught to sing Erin's dark bondage and woes
And the breath of the bugle now wafted them o'er
From Dinis' green isle to Glenà's wooded shore.

* Written during a visit to Lord Kenmare, at Killarney.

He listen'd — while high o'er the eagle's rude nest,
The lingering sounds on their way lov'd to rest;
And the echoes sung back from their full mountain
    quire,
As if loth to let song so enchanting expire.

It seem'd as if every sweet note that died here
Was again brought to life in some airier sphere,
Some heaven in those hills, where the soul of the strain
That had ceas'd upon earth was awaking again.

Oh forgive, if, while listening to music, whose breath
Seem'd to circle his name with a charm against death,
He should feel a proud Spirit within him proclaim,
" Even so shalt thou live in the echoes of Fame:

" Even so, tho' thy memory should now die away
" 'T will be caught up again in some happier day,
" And the hearts and the voices of Erin prolong,
" Thro' the answering future, thy name and thy song."

FAIREST! PUT ON AWHILE.

FAIREST! put on awhile
    These pinions of light I bring thee,
And o'er thy own green isle
    In fancy let me wing thee.
Never did Ariel's plume,
    At golden sunset, hover
O'er scenes so full of bloom
    As I shall waft thee over.

Fields, where the Spring delays,
   And fearlessly meets the ardor
Of the warm Summer's gaze,
   With only her tears to guard her.
Rocks, through myrtle boughs
   In grace majestic frowning;
Like some bold warrior's brows
   That Love hath just been crowning.

Islets, so freshly fair,
   That never hath bird come nigh them,
But from his course through air
   He hath been won down by them—*
Types, sweet maid, of thee,
   Whose look, whose blush inviting,
Never did Love yet see
   From heaven, without alighting.

Lakes, where the pearl lies hid,†
   And caves, where the gem is sleeping,
Bright as the tears thy lid
   Lets fall in lonely weeping.

---

* In describing the Skeligs (islands in the Barony of Forth), Dr. Keating says, "There is a certain attractive virtue in the soil which draws down all the birds that attempt to fly over it, and obliges them to light upon the rock."

† "Nennius, a British writer of the ninth century, mentions the abundance of pearls in Ireland. Their princes, he says, hung them behind their ears; and this we find confirmed by a present made A.C. 1094, by Gilbert, bishop of Limerick, to Anselm, archbishop of Canterbury, of a considerable quantity of Irish pearls."—O'HALLORAN.

Glens,* where Ocean comes,
  To 'scape the wild wind's rancour,
And harbours, worthiest homes
  Where Freedom's fleet can anchor.

Then if, while scenes so grand,
  So beautiful, shine before thee,
Pride for thy own dear land
  Should haply be stealing o'er thee,
Oh, let grief come first,
  O'er pride itself victorious —
Thinking how man hath curst
  What Heaven had made so glorious.

QUICK! WE HAVE BUT A SECOND.

QUICK! we have but a second,
  Fill round the cup, while you may:
For Time, the churl, hath beckon'd,
  And we must away, away!
Grasp the pleasure that's flying,
  For oh! not Orpheus' strain
Could keep sweet hours from dying,
  Or charm them to life again.
    Then, quick! we have but a second,
      Fill round the cup, while you may;
    For Time, the churl, hath beckon'd,
      And we must away, away!

* Glengariff.

See the glass, how it flushes,
   Like some young Hebe's lip,
And half meets thine, and blushes
   That thou shouldst delay to sip.
Shame, oh shame unto thee,
   If ever thou seest that day,
When a cup or a lip shall woo thee,
   And turn untouch'd away!
      Then quick! we have but a second,
         Fill round, fill round, while you may,
      For Time, the churl, hath beckon'd,
         And we must away, away!

AND DOTH NOT A MEETING LIKE THIS.

AND doth not a meeting like this make amends
   For all the long years I've been wand'ring away—
To see thus around me my youth's early friends,
   As smiling and kind as in that happy day?
Though haply o'er some of your brows, as o'er mine,
   The snow-fall of time may be stealing—what then?
Like Alps in the sun-set, thus lighted by wine,
   We'll wear the gay tinge of youth's roses again.

What soften'd remembrances come o'er the heart,
   In gazing on those we've been lost to so long!
The sorrows, the joys, of which once they were part,
   Still round them, like visions of yesterday, throng.
As letters some hand hath invisibly traced,
   When held to the flame will steal out on the sight,

So many a feeling, that long seem'd effaced,
　　The warmth of a moment like this brings to light.

And thus, as in memory's bark we shall glide
　　To visit the scenes of our boyhood anew,
Though oft we may see, looking down on the tide,
　　The wreck of full many a hope shining through;
Yet still, as in fancy we point to the flowers
　　That once made a garden of all the gay shore,
Deceiv'd for a moment, we'll think them still ours,
　　And breathe the fresh air of life's morning once
　　　　more.*

So brief our existence, a glimpse, at the most,
　　Is all we can have of the few we hold dear;
And oft even joy is unheeded and lost,
　　For want of some heart, that could echo it, near.
Ah, well may we hope, when this short life is gone,
　　To meet in some world of more permanent bliss;
For a smile, or a grasp of the hand, hastening on,
　　Is all we enjoy of each other in this.†

---

* " Jours charmans, quand je songe à vos heureux instans,
　　Je pense remonter le fleuve de mes ans;
　　Et mon cœur enchanté sur la rive fleurie
　　Respire encore l'air pur du matin de la vie."

† The same thought has been happily expressed by my friend Mr. Washington Irving, in his 'Bracebridge Hall,' vol. i. p. 213. The pleasure which I feel in calling this gentleman my friend is much enhanced by the reflection, that he is too good an American to have admitted me so readily to such a distinction, if he had not known that my feelings towards the great and free country that gave him birth have long been such as every real lover of the liberty and happiness of the human race must entertain.

But, come, the more rare such delights to the heart,
　The more we should welcome and bless them the more,
They're ours, when we meet,— they are lost, when we part,
　Like birds that bring summer and fly when 't is o'er.
Thus circling the cup, hand in hand, ere we drink,
　Let Sympathy pledge us, thro' pleasure, thro' pain,
That, fast as a feeling but touches one link,
　Her magic shall send it direct through the chain.

THE MOUNTAIN SPRITE.

IN yonder valley there dwelt, alone,
　A youth whose moments had calmly flown,
Till spells came o'er him, and, day and night,
He was haunted and watch'd by a Mountain Sprite.

As once, by moonlight, he wander'd o'er
The golden sands of that island shore,
A foot-print sparkled before his sight —
'T was the fairy foot of the Mountain Sprite!

Beside a fountain, one sunny day,
As bending over the stream he lay,
There peep'd down o'er him two eyes of light,
And he saw, in that mirror, the Mountain Sprite.

He turn'd — but, lo, like a startled bird,
That spirit fled — and the youth but heard
Sweet music, such as marks the flight
Of some bird of song, from the Mountain Sprite.

One night, still haunted by that bright look,
The boy, bewilder'd, his pencil took,
And, guided only by memory's light,
Drew the once-seen form of the Mountain Sprite.

"Oh thou, who lovest the shadow," cried
A voice, low whispering by his side,
"Now turn and see,"—here the youth's delight
Seal'd the rosy lips of the Mountain Sprite.

"Of all the Spirits of land and sea,"
Then rapt he murmur'd, "there's none like thee,
"And oft, oh oft, may thy foot thus light
"In this lonely bower, sweet Mountain Sprite!"

AS VANQUISH'D ERIN.

AS vanquish'd Erin wept beside
   The Boyne's ill-fated river,
She saw where Discord, in the tide,
   Had dropt his loaded quiver.
"Lie hid," she cried, "ye venom'd darts,
   "Where mortal eye may shun you;
"Lie hid—the stain of manly hearts
   "That bled for me is on you."

But vain her wish, her weeping vain,—
   As Time too well hath taught her—
Each year the Fiend returns again,
   And dives into that water;

And brings triumphant from beneath
   His shafts of desolation,
And sends them, wing'd with worse than death,
   Through all her madd'ning nation.

Alas for her who sits and mourns,
   Even now, beside that river —
Unwearied still the Fiend returns,
   And stor'd is still his quiver,
" When will this end, ye Powers of Good ?"
   She weeping asks for ever ;
But only hears, from out that flood,
   The demon answer, " Never !"

DESMOND'S SONG.*

BY the Feal's wave benighted,
   No star in the skies,
To thy door by Love lighted,
   I first saw those eyes.

---

* " Thomas, the heir of the Desmond family, had accidentally been so engaged in the chase, that he was benighted near Tralee, and obliged to take shelter at the Abbey of Feal, in the house of one of his dependents, called Mac Cormac. Catherine, a beautiful daughter of his host, instantly inspired the Earl with a violent passion, which he could not subdue. He married her, and by this inferior alliance alienated his followers, whose brutal pride regarded this indulgence of his love as an unpardonable degradation of his family."—LELAND, vol. ii.

Some voice whisper'd o'er me,
  As the threshold I crost,
There was ruin before me,
  If I lov'd I was lost.

Love came, and brought sorrow
  Too soon in his train;
Yet so sweet, that to-morrow
  'T were welcome again.
Though misery's full measure
  My portion should be,
I would drain it with pleasure,
  If pour'd out by thee.

You, who call it dishonour
  To bow to this flame,
If you've eyes, look but on her,
  And blush while you blame.
Hath the pearl less whiteness
  Because of its birth?
Hath the violet less brightness
  For growing near earth?

No—Man for his glory
  To ancestry flies;
But Woman's bright story
  Is told in her eyes.
While the Monarch but traces
  Through mortals his line,
Beauty, born of the Graces,
  Ranks next to Divine!

THEY KNOW NOT MY HEART.

THEY know not my heart, who believe there can be
  One stain of this earth in its feelings for thee;
Who think, while I see thee in beauty's young hour,
As pure as the morning's first dew on the flower,
I could harm what I love — as the sun's wanton ray
But smiles on the dew-drop to waste it away.

No — beaming with light as those young features are,
There's a light round thy heart which is lovelier far:
It *is* not that cheek — 't is the soul dawning clear
Through its innocent blush makes thy beauty so dear;
As the sky we look up to, though glorious and fair,
Is look'd up to the more, because heaven lies there!

I WISH I WAS BY THAT DIM LAKE.

I WISH I was by that dim Lake*
  Where sinful souls their farewell take
Of this vain world, and half-way lie
In death's cold shadow, ere they die.

* These verses are meant to allude to that ancient haunt of superstition, called Patrick's Purgatory. "In the midst of these gloomy regions of Donegal (says Dr. Campbell) lay a lake, which was to become the mystic theatre of this fabled and intermediate state. In the lake were several islands; but one of them was dignified with that called the Mouth of Purgatory, which, during the dark ages attracted the notice of all Christendom, and was the

There, there, far from thee,
Deceitful world, my home should be ;
Where, come what might of gloom and pain,
False hope should ne'er deceive again.

The lifeless sky, the mournful sound
Of unseen waters falling round ;
The dry leaves, quivering o'er my head,
Like man, unquiet even when dead ;
These, ay, these shall wean
My soul from life's deluding scene,
And turn each thought, o'ercharg'd with gloom,
Like willows, downward tow'rds the tomb.

As they, who to their couch at night
Would win repose, first quench the light,
So must the hopes, that keep this breast
Awake, be quench'd, ere it can rest.
Cold, cold, this heart must grow,
Unmov'd by either joy or woe,
Like freezing founts, where all that's thrown
Within their current turns to stone.

---

resort of penitents and pilgrims from almost every country in Europe."

" It was," as the same writer tells us, " one of the most dismal and dreary spots in the North, almost inaccessible, through deep glens and rugged mountains, frightful with impending rocks, and the hollow murmurs of the western winds in dark caverns, peopled only with such fantastic beings as the mind, however gay, is, from strange association, wont to appropriate to such gloomy scenes."—*Strict. on the Eccl. and Lit. Hist. of Ireland.*

SHE SUNG OF LOVE.

SHE sung of Love, while o'er her lyre
    The rosy rays of evening fell,
As if to feed with their soft fire
    The soul within that trembling shell.
The same rich light hung o'er her cheek,
    And play'd around those lips that sung
And spoke, as flowers would sing and speak,
    If Love could lend their leaves a tongue.

But soon the West no longer burn'd;
    Each rosy ray from heaven withdrew;
And when to gaze again I turn'd,
    The minstrel's form seem'd fading too.
As if *her* light and heaven's were one,
    The glory all had left that frame;
And from her glimmering lips the tone,
    As from a parting spirit, came.*

Who ever lov'd, but had the thought
    That he and all he lov'd must part?
Fill'd with this fear, I flew and caught
    The fading image to my heart —

---

* The thought here was suggested by some beautiful lines in Mr. Rogers's Poem of "Human Life," beginning —

    "Now in the glimmering, dying light she grows
      Less and less earthly."

I would quote the entire passage, but that I fear to put my own humble imitation of it out of countenance.

And cried, " Oh Love ! is this thy doom ?
  " Oh light of youth's resplendent day !
" Must ye then lose your golden bloom,
  " And thus, like sunshine, die away ? "

SING — SING — MUSIC WAS GIVEN.

SING — sing — Music was given
  To brighten the gay, and kindle the loving ;
Souls here, like planets in heaven,
  By harmony's laws alone are kept moving.
Beauty may boast of her eyes and her cheeks,
  But Love from the lips his true archery wings ;
And she, who but feathers the dart when she speaks,
  At once sends it home to the heart when she sings.
    Then sing — sing — Music was given
      To brighten the gay, and kindle the loving ;
    Souls here, like planets in heaven,
      By harmony's laws alone are kept moving.

When Love, rock'd by his mother,
  Lay sleeping, as calm as slumber could make him,
" Hush, hush," said Venus, " no other
  Sweet voice but his own is worthy to wake him."
Dreaming of music he slumber'd the while,
  Till faint from his lip a soft melody broke,
And Venus, enchanted, look'd on with a smile,
  While Love to his own sweet singing awoke.

Then sing — sing — Music was given
  To brighten the gay, and kindle the loving;
Souls here, like planets in heaven,
  By harmony's laws alone are kept moving.

THOUGH HUMBLE THE BANQUET.

THO' humble the banquet to which I invite thee,
  Thou 'lt find there the best a poor bard can command:
Eyes, beaming with welcome, shall throng round, to light thee,
  And Love serve the feast with his own willing hand.

And though Fortune may seem to have turn'd from the dwelling
  Of him thou regardest her favouring ray,
Thou wilt find there a gift, all her treasures excelling,
  Which, proudly he feels, hath ennobled his way.

'Tis that freedom of mind which no vulgar dominion
  Can turn from the path a pure conscience approves;
Which, with hope in the heart, and no chain on the pinion,
  Holds upwards its course to the light which it loves.

'T is this makes the pride of his humble retreat,
  And, with this, tho' of all other treasures bereav'd,
The breeze of his garden to him is more sweet
  Than the costliest incense that Pomp e'er receiv'd.

Then come, — if a board so untempting hath power
  To win thee from grandeur, its best shall be thine;
And there's one, long the light of the bard's happy
    bower,
  Who, smiling, will blend her bright welcome with
    mine.

SING, SWEET HARP.

SING, sweet Harp, oh sing to me
  Some song of ancient days,
Whose sounds, in this sad memory,
  Long buried dreams shall raise; —
Some lay that tells of vanish'd fame,
  Whose light once round us shone;
Of noble pride now turn'd to shame,
  And hopes for ever gone. —
Sing, sad Harp, thus sing to me;
  Alike our doom is cast,
Both lost to all but memory,
  We live but in the past.

How mournfully the midnight air
  Among thy chords doth sigh,
As if it sought some echo there
  Of voices long gone by; —
Of chieftains now forgot, who seem'd
  The foremost then in fame;
Of bards who, once immortal deem'd,
  Now sleep without a name! —

In vain, sad Harp, the midnight air
    Among thy chords doth sigh;
In vain it seeks an echo there
    Of voices long gone by.

Couldst thou but call those spirits round,
    Who once, in bower and hall,
Sate listening to thy magic sound,
    Now mute and mouldering all;
But, no; they would but wake to weep
    Their children's slavery;
Then leave them in their dreamless sleep,
    The dead, at least, are free. —
Hush, hush, sad Harp, that dreary tone,
    That knell of Freedom's day,
Or, listening to its death-like moan,
    Let me, too, die away.

SONG OF THE BATTLE EVE.

TIME — THE NINTH CENTURY.

TO-MORROW, comrade, we
    On the battle-plain must be,
There to conquer, or both lie low!
    The morning-star is up, —
    But there's wine still in the cup,
And we'll take another quaff, ere we go, boy, go;
We'll take another quaff, ere we go.

'T is true, in manliest eyes
A passing tear will rise,
When we think of the friends we leave lone ;
But what can wailing do ?
See, our goblet's weeping too !
With its tears we'll chase away our own, boy,
   our own ;
With its tears we'll chase away our own.

But daylight's stealing on ;—
The last that o'er us shone
Saw our children around us play ;
The next—ah ! where shall we
And those rosy urchins be ?
But—no matter—grasp thy sword and away, boy,
   away.
No matter — grasp thy sword, and away !

Let those who brook the chain
Of Saxon or of Dane
Ignobly by their fire-sides stay ;
One sigh to home be given,
One heartfelt prayer to heaven,
Then, for Erin and her cause, boy, hurra ! hurra !
   hurra !
Then, for Erin and her cause, hurra !

THE WANDERING BARD.

WHAT life like that of the bard can be,
  The wandering bard, who roams as free
As the mountain lark that o'er him sings,
And, like that lark, a music brings
Within him, where'er he comes or goes, —
A fount that for ever flows ! —
The world's to him like some play-ground,
Where fairies dance their moonlight round;
If dimm'd the turf where late they trod,
The elves but seek some greener sod:
So, when less bright his scene of glee,
To another away flies he.

Oh, what would have been young Beauty's doom,
Without a bard to fix her bloom?
They tell us, in the moon's bright round,
Things lost in this dark world are found;
So charms, on earth long pass'd and gone,
In the poet's lay live on. —
Would ye have smiles that ne'er grow dim?
You've only to give them all to him,
Who, with a touch of Fancy's wand,
Can lend them life, this life beyond,
And fix them high, in Poesy's sky, —
Young stars that never die.

Then, welcome the bard where'er he comes,
For, though he hath countless airy homes,

To which his wing excursive roves,
Yet still, from time to time he loves
To light upon earth and find such cheer
As brightens our banquet here.
No matter how far, how fleet he flies,
You've only to light up kind young eyes,
Such signal-fires as here are given, —
And down he'll drop from Fancy's heaven,
The minute such call to love or mirth
Proclaims he's wanting on earth.

ALONE IN CROWDS TO WANDER ON.

ALONE in crowds to wander on,
  And feel that all the charm is gone
Which voices dear and eyes belov'd
Shed round us once, where'er we rov'd —
This, this the doom must be
Of all who've lov'd, and liv'd to see
The few bright things, they thought would stay
For ever near them, die away.

Though fairer forms around us throng,
Their smiles to others all belong,
And want that charm which dwells alone
Round those the fond heart calls its own.
Where, where the sunny brow?
The long-known voice—where are they now?
Thus ask I still, nor ask in vain,
The silence answers all too plain.

Oh what is Fancy's magic worth,
If all her art cannot call forth
One bliss like those we felt of old
From lips now mute, and eyes now cold!
No, no, — her spell is vain, —
As soon could she bring back again
Those eyes themselves from out the grave,
As wake again one bliss they gave

I'VE A SECRET TO TELL THEE.

I'VE a secret to tell thee, but hush! not here, —
   Oh! not where the world its vigil keeps:
I'll seek, to whisper it in thine ear,
   Some shore where the Spirit of Silence sleeps;
Where summer's wave unmurmuring dies,
   Nor fay can hear the fountain's gush;
Where, if but a note her night-bird sighs,
   The rose saith, chidingly, "Hush, sweet, hush!"

There, amid the deep silence of that hour,
   When stars can be heard in ocean dip,
Thyself shall, under some rosy bower,
   Sit mute, with thy finger on thy lip:
Like him, the boy,[*] who born among
   The flowers that on the Nile-stream blush,
Sits ever thus,—his only song
   To earth and heaven, "Hush, all, hush!"

[*] The God of Silence, thus pictured by the Egyptians.

SONG OF INNISFAIL.

THEY came from a land beyond the sea,
    And now o'er the western main
Set sail, in their good ships, gallantly,
    From the sunny land of Spain.
" Oh, where's the Isle we've seen in dreams,
    Our destin'd home or grave ?" *
Thus sung they as, by the morning's beams,
    They swept the Atlantic wave.

And, lo, where afar o'er ocean shines
    A sparkle of radiant green,
As though in that deep lay emerald mines,
    Whose light through the wave was seen.
" 'T is Innisfail — 't is Innisfail !" †
    Rings o'er the echoing sea,
While, bending to heaven, the warriors hail
    That home of the brave and free.

Then turn'd they unto the Eastern wave,
    Where now their Day-God's eye
A look of such sunny omen gave
    As lighted up sea and sky.
Nor frown was seen through sky or sea,
    Nor tear o'er leaf or sod,
When first on their Isle of Destiny
    Our great forefathers trod.

* " Milesius remembered the remarkable prediction of the principal Druid, who foretold that the posterity of Gadelus should obtain the possession of a Western Island (which was Ireland), and there inhabit."—KEATING.
† The Island of Destiny, one of the ancient names of Ireland.

THE NIGHT DANCE.

STRIKE the gay harp! see the moon is on high,
   And, as true to her beam as the tides of the ocean,
Young hearts, when they feel the soft light of her eye,
   Obey the mute call, and heave into motion.
Then sound notes — the gayest, the lightest,
That ever took wing, when heaven look'd brightest!
        Again! Again!
Oh! could such heart-stirring music be heard
   In that City of Statues described by romancers,
So wakening its spell, even stone would be stirr'd,
   And statues themselves all start into dancers!

Why then delay, with such sounds in our ears,
   And the flower of Beauty's own garden before us,—
While stars overhead leave the song of their spheres,
   And, list'ning to ours, hang wond'ring o'er us?
Again, that strain! — to hear it thus sounding
Might set even Death's cold pulses bounding —
        Again! Again!
Oh, what delight when the youthful and gay,
   Each with eye like a sunbeam and foot like a feather,
Thus dance, like the Hours to the music of May,
   And mingle sweet song and sunshine together!

THERE ARE SOUNDS OF MIRTH.

THERE are sounds of mirth in the night-air ringing.
    And lamps from every casement shown;
While voices blithe within are singing,
    That seem to say "Come," in every tone.
Ah! once how light, in Life's young season,
    My heart had leap'd at that sweet lay;
Nor paus'd to ask of greybeard Reason
    Should I the siren call obey.

And see—the lamps still livelier glitter,
    The siren lips more fondly sound;
No, seek, ye nymphs, some victim fitter
    To sink in your rosy bondage bound.
Shall a bard whom not the world in arms
    Could bend to tyranny's rude control,
Thus quail at sight of woman's charms,
    And yield to a smile his freeborn soul?

Thus sung the sage, while, slyly stealing,
    The nymphs their fetters around him cast,
And,—their laughing eyes, the while, concealing,—
    Led Freedom's Bard their slave at last.
For the Poet's heart, still prone to loving,
    Was like that rock of the Druid race,*
Which the gentlest touch at once set moving,
    But all earth's power could n't cast from its base.

* The Rocking Stones of the Druids, some of which no force is able to dislodge from their stations.

OH ARRANMORE, LOVED ARRANMORE.

OH! Arranmore, lov'd Arranmore,
   How oft I dream of thee,
And of those days when, by thy shore,
   I wander'd young and free.
Full many a path I've tried, since then,
   Through pleasure's flowery maze,
But ne'er could find the bliss again
   I felt in those sweet days.

How blithe upon thy breezy cliffs
   At sunny morn I've stood,
With heart as bounding as the skiffs
   That danc'd along thy flood;
Or, when the western wave grew bright
   With daylight's parting wing,
Have sought that Eden in its light
   Which dreaming poets sing;—*

That Eden, where the immortal brave
   Dwell in a land serene,—
Whose bowers beyond the shining wave,
   At sunset, oft are seen.

---

* "The inhabitants of Arranmore are still persuaded that, in a clear day, they can see from this coast Hy Brysail, or the Enchanted Island, the Paradise of the Pagan Irish, and concerning which they relate a number of romantic stories."—BEAUFORT'S Ancient Topography of Ireland.

Ah dream too full of saddening truth!
   Those mansions o'er the main
Are like the hopes I built in youth,—
   As sunny and as vain!

LAY HIS SWORD BY HIS SIDE.

LAY his sword by his side,*—it hath serv'd him too well,
   Not to rest near his pillow below;
To the last moment true, from his hand ere it fell,
   Its point was still turn'd to a flying foe.
Fellow-laborers in life, let them slumber in death,
   Side by side, as becomes the reposing brave, —
That sword which he lov'd still unbroke in its sheath,
   And himself unsubdued in his grave.

Yet pause — for, in fancy, a still voice I hear,
   As if breath'd from his brave heart's remains;—
Faint echo of that which, in Slavery's ear,
   Once sounded the war-word, "Burst your chains!"
And it cries, from the grave where the hero lies deep,
   "Tho' the day of your Chieftain for ever hath set,
"Oh leave not his sword thus inglorious to sleep, —
   "It hath victory's life in it yet!

* It was the custom of the ancient Irish, in the manner of the Scythians, to bury the favorite swords of their heroes along with them.

"Should some alien, unworthy such weapon to wield,
   "Dare to touch thee, my own gallant sword,
"Then rest in thy sheath, like a talisman seal'd,
   "Or return to the grave of thy chainless lord.
"But, if grasp'd by a hand that hath learn'd the proud use
   "Of a falchion like thee on the battle-plain,—
"Then, at Liberty's summons, like lightning let loose,
   "Leap forth from thy dark sheath again!"

OH, COULD WE DO WITH THIS WORLD.

OH could we do with this world of ours
   As thou dost with thy garden bowers,
Reject the weeds and keep the flowers,
   What a heaven on earth we'd make it!
So bright a dwelling should be our own,
So warranted free from sigh or frown,
That angels soon would be coming down,
   By the week or month to take it.

Like those gay flies that wing through air,
And in themselves a lustre bear,
A stock of light, still ready there,
   Whenever they wish to use it;
So in this world I'd make for thee,
Our hearts should all like fire-flies be,
And the flash of wit or poesy
   Break forth whenever we choose it.

And even of the light which Hope once shed o'er thy chains,
Alas, not a gleam to grace thy freedom remains.

Say, is it that slavery sunk so deep in thy heart,
That still the dark brand is there, though chainless thou art ;
And Freedom's sweet fruit, for which thy spirit long burn'd,
Now, reaching at last thy lip, to ashes hath turn'd ?

Up Liberty's steep by Truth and Eloquence led,
With eyes on her temple fix'd, how proud was thy tread !
Ah, better thou ne'er hadst liv'd that summit to gain,
Or died in the porch, than thus dishonour the fane.

FROM THIS HOUR THE PLEDGE IS GIVEN.

FROM this hour the pledge is given,
　　From this hour my soul is thine :
Come what will, from earth or heaven,
　　Weal or woe, thy fate be mine !
When the proud and great stood by thee,
　　None dar'd thy rights to spurn ;
And, if now they're false and fly thee,
　　Shall I, too, basely turn ?
No ;—whate'er the fires that try thee,
　　In the same this heart shall burn.

Though the sea, where thou embarkest,
  Offers now no friendly shore,
Light may come where all looks darkest,
  Hope hath life, when life seems o'er.
And of those past ages dreaming,
  When glory deck'd thy brow,
Oft I fondly think, though seeming
  So fallen and clouded now,
Thou'lt again break forth, all beaming,—
  None so bright, so blest as thou.

SILENCE IS IN OUR FESTAL HALLS.*

SILENCE is in our festal halls,—
  Sweet Son of Song! thy course is o'er:
In vain on thee sad Erin calls,
  Her minstrel's voice responds no more;—
All silent as th' Eolian shell
  Sleeps at the close of some bright day,
When the sweet breeze, that wak'd its swell
  At sunny morn hath died away.

Yet at our feasts thy spirit long
  Awak'd by music's spell shall rise;

---

* It is hardly necessary, perhaps, to inform the reader, that these lines are meant as a tribute of sincere friendship to the memory of an old and valued colleague in this work, Sir John Stevenson.

For name so link'd with deathless song
   Partakes its charm and never dies:
And even within the holy fane,
   When music wafts the soul to heaven,
One thought of him, whose earliest strain
   Was echo'd there, shall long be given.

But, where is now the cheerful day,
   The social night, when, by thy side,
He, who now weaves this parting lay,
   His skilless voice with thine allied;
And sung those songs whose every tone,
   When bard and minstrel long have past.
Shall still, in sweetness all their own,
   Embalm'd by fame, undying last.

Yes, Erin, thine alone the fame, —
   Or, if thy bard have shar'd the crown,
From thee the borrow'd glory came,
   And at thy feet is now laid down.
Enough, if Freedom still inspire
   His latest song, and still there be,
As evening closes round his lyre,
   One ray upon its chords from thee.

SACRED SONGS.

SACRED SONGS.

THOU ART, OH GOD!

"The day is thine; the night also is thine: thou hast prepared the light and the sun. Thou hast set all the borders of the earth; thou hast made summer and winter."—PSA. lxxiv. 16, 17.

THOU art, O God! the life and light
   Of all this wondrous world we see.
Its glow by day, its smile by night,
   Are but reflections caught from thee.
Where'er we turn, thy glories shine,
And all things fair and bright are Thine!

When Day, with farewell beam, delays
   Among the opening clouds of Even,
And we can almost think we gaze
   Through golden vistas into heaven —
Those hues, that make the sun's decline
So soft, so radiant, Lord! are Thine.

When Night, with wings of starry gloom,
   O'ershadows all the earth and skies,
Like some dark, beauteous bird, whose plume
   Is sparkling with unnumbered eyes —
That sacred gloom, those fires divine,
So grand, so countless, Lord! are Thine.

When youthful Spring around us breathes,
   Thy Spirit warms her fragrant sigh ;
And every flower the Summer wreathes
   Is born beneath that kindling eye.
Where'er we turn, thy glories shine,
And all things fair and bright are Thine !

FALLEN IS THY THRONE.

FALLEN is thy throne, O Israel !
   Silence is o'er thy plains ;
Thy dwellings all lie desolate,
   Thy children weep in chains.
Where are the dews that fed thee
   On Etham's barren shore ?
That fire from heaven which led thee,
   Now lights thy path no more.

Lord ! thou didst love Jerusalem —
   Once she was all thy own ;
Her love thy fairest heritage,*
   Her power thy glory's throne ;†
Till evil came, and blighted
   Thy long-loved olive-tree ;‡
And Salem's shrines were lighted
   For other gods than Thee !

---

* " I have left mine heritage ; I have given the dearly-beloved of my soul into the hands of her enemies."—JER. xii. 7.

† " Do not disgrace the throne of thy glory."—JER. xiv. 21.

‡ " The Lord called thy name a green olive-tree ; fair and of goodly fruit."—JER. xi. 16.

Then sunk the star of Solyma—
  Then pass'd her glory's day,
Like heath that, in the wilderness,§
  The wild wind whirls away.
Silent and waste her bowers,
  Where once the mighty trod,
And sunk those guilty towers,
  While Baal reign'd as God!

"Go,"—said the Lord—"Ye conquerors
  Steep in her blood your swords,
And rase to earth her battlements,*
  For they are not the Lord's!
Till Zion's mournful daughter
  O'er kindred bones shall tread,
And Hinnom's vale of slaughter †
  Shall hide but half her dead."

THIS WORLD IS ALL A FLEETING SHOW.

THIS world is all a fleeting show,
    For man's illusion given;
The smiles of Joy, the tears of Woe,

§ "For he shall be like the heath in the desert."—JER. xvii. 6.
* "Take away her battlements; for they are not the Lord's."—JER. v. 10.
† "Therefore, behold, the days come, saith the Lord, that it shall no more be called Tophet, nor the Valley of the Son of Hinnom, but the Valley of Slaughter; for they shall bury in Tophet, till there be no place."—JER. vii. 32.

Deceitful shine, deceitful flow—
   There's nothing true but heaven!

And false the light on Glory's plume,
   As fading hues of Even;
And Love, and Hope, and Beauty's bloom
Are blossoms gather'd for the tomb,—
   There's nothing bright but heaven.

Poor wanderers of a stormy day,
   From wave to wave we're driven,
And Fancy's flash, and Reason's ray,
Serve but to light the troubled way —
   There's nothing calm but heaven!

WHO IS THE MAID?

ST. JEROME'S LOVE.[*]

WHO is the maid my spirit seeks,
   Through cold reproof and slander's blight?
Has *she* Love's roses on her cheeks?
   Is *her*'s an eye of this world's light?
No, — wan and sunk with midnight prayer
   Are the pale looks of her I love;

---

[*] These lines were suggested by a passage in St. Jerome's reply to some calumnious remarks that had been circulated upon his intimacy with the matron Paula :—" Numquid me vestes sericæ, nitentes gemma, picta facies, aut auri rapuit ambitio? Nulla fuit alia Romæ matronarum, quæ meam possit edomare mentem, nisi lugens atque jejunans, fletu pene cæcata."—Epist. 'Si tibi putem.'

Or if, at times, a light be there,
  Its beam is kindled from above.

I chose not her, my soul's elect,
  From those who seek their Maker's shrine
In gems and garlands proudly deck'd,
  As if themselves were things divine!
No—Heaven but faintly warms the breast
  That beats beneath a broider'd veil;
And she who comes in glittering vest
  To mourn her frailty, still is frail.†

Not so the faded form I prize
  And love, because its bloom is gone;
The glory in those sainted eyes
  Is all the grace her brow puts on.
And ne'er was Beauty's dawn so bright,
  So touching as that form's decay,
Which, like the altar's trembling light,
  In holy lustre wastes away!

THE BIRD LET LOOSE.

THE bird, let loose in eastern skies,‡
  When hastening fondly home,
Ne'er stoops to earth her wing, nor flies
  Where idle warblers roam.

† Chrysost. Homil. 8. in Epist. ad Tim.

‡ The carrier-pigeon, it is well known, flies at an elevated pitch, in order to surmount every obstacle between her and the place to which she is destined.

But high she shoots through air and light,
  Above all low delay,
Where nothing earthly bounds her flight,
  Nor shadow dims her way.

So grant me, God! from every care
  And stain of passion free,
Aloft, through Virtue's purer air,
  To hold my course to Thee!
No sin to cloud — no lure to stay
  My Soul, as home she springs;—
Thy sunshine on her joyful way,
  Thy freedom in her wings!

OH THOU WHO DRY'ST!

"He healeth the broken in heart, and bindeth up their wounds."
—Psa. cxlvii. 3.

OH Thou! who dry'st the mourner's tear,
  How dark this world would be,
If, when deceiv'd and wounded here,
  We could not fly to Thee!
The friends who in our sunshine live,
  When winter comes, are flown;
And he, who has but tears to give,
  Must weep those tears alone.
But Thou wilt heal that broken heart,
  Which, like the plants that throw
Their fragrance from the wounded part,
  Breathes sweetness out of woe.

When joy no longer soothes or cheers,
　　And even the hope that threw
A moment's sparkle o'er our tears,
　　Is dimm'd and vanish'd too!
Oh! who would bear life's stormy doom,
　　Did not thy wing of love
Come, brightly wafting through the gloom
　　Our peace-branch from above?
Then sorrow, touch'd by Thee, grows bright
　　With more than rapture's ray;
As darkness shows us worlds of light
　　We never saw by day!

WEEP NOT FOR THOSE.

WEEP not for those whom the veil of the tomb,
　　In life's happy morning, hath hid from our eyes,
Ere sin threw a blight o'er the spirit's young bloom,
　　Or earth had profaned what was born for the skies.
Death chill'd the fair fountain ere sorrow had stain'd it,
'Twas frozen in all the pure light of its course,
And but sleeps till the sunshine of heaven has unchain'd it,
　　To water that Eden where first was its source!
Weep not for those whom the veil of the tomb,
　　In life's happy morning, hath hid from our eyes,
Ere sin threw a blight o'er the spirit's young bloom,
　　Or earth had profaned what was born for the skies.

Mourn not for her, the young Bride of the Vale,*
  Our gayest and loveliest, lost to us now,
Ere life's early lustre had time to grow pale,
  And the garland of love was yet fresh on her brow!
Oh! then was her moment, dear spirit, for flying
  From this gloomy world, while its gloom was unknown —
And the wild hymns she warbled so sweetly, in dying,
  Were echoed in heaven by lips like her own!
Weep not for her, — in her spring-time she flew
  To that land where the wings of the soul are unfurl'd,
And now, like a star beyond evening's cold dew,
  Looks radiantly down on the tears of this world.

THE TURF SHALL BE MY FRAGRANT SHRINE.

THE turf shall be my fragrant shrine;
  My temple, Lord! that arch of thine;
My censer's breath the mountain airs,
And silent thoughts my only prayers.†

---

* This second verse, which I wrote long after the first, alludes to the fate of a very lovely and amiable girl, the daughter of the late Colonel Bainbrigge, who was married in Ashbourne church, October 31, 1815, and died of a fever in a few weeks after: the sound of her marriage bells seeming scarcely out of our ears when we heard of her death. During her last delirium she sung several hymns, in a voice even clearer and sweeter than usual, and among them were some from the present collection (particularly, "There's nothing bright but Heaven,") which this very interesting girl had often heard during the summer.

† Pii orant tacite.

My choir shall be the moonlight waves,
When murmuring homeward to their caves,
Or when the stillness of the sea,
Even more than music, breathes of Thee!

I'll seek, by day, some glade unknown,
All light and silence, like thy throne!
And the pale stars shall be, at night,
The only eyes that watch my rite.

Thy heaven, on which 't is bliss to look,
Shall be my pure and shining book,
Where I shall read, in words of flame,
The glories of thy wondrous name.

I'll read thy anger in the rack
That clouds awhile the day-beam's track;
Thy mercy in the azure hue
Of sunny brightness breaking through!

There's nothing bright, above, below,
From flowers that bloom to stars that glow,
But in its light my soul can see
Some feature of the Deity!

There's nothing dark, below, above,
But in its gloom I trace thy love,
And meekly wait that moment when
Thy touch shall turn all bright again!

SOUND THE LOUD TIMBREL.

MIRIAM'S SONG.

"And Miriam, the Prophetess, the sister of Aaron, took a timbrel in her hand; and all the women went out after her with timbrels and with dances."—Exod. xv. 20.

SOUND the loud timbrel o'er Egypt's dark sea!
  Jehovah has triumph'd—his people are free.
Sing — for the pride of the tyrant is broken,
  His chariots, his horsemen, all splendid and brave;
How vain was their boast, for the Lord hath but spoken,
  And chariots and horsemen are sunk in the wave.
Sound the loud timbrel o'er Egypt's dark sea!
Jehovah has triumph'd,—his people are free!

Praise to the Conqueror, praise to the Lord!
His word was our arrow, his breath was our sword!—
Who shall return to tell Egypt the story
  Of those she sent forth in the hour of her pride?
For the Lord hath look'd out from his pillar of glory,*
And all her brave thousands are dashed in the tide!
Sound the loud timbrel o'er Egypt's dark sea!
Jehovah has triumph'd,— his people are free.

---

* "And it came to pass, that, in the morning-watch, the Lord looked unto the host of the Egyptians, through the pillar of fire and of the cloud, and troubled the hosts of the Egyptians."—Exod. xiv. 24.

GO, LET ME WEEP!

GO, let me weep — there's bliss in tears,
    When he who sheds them inly feels
Some ling'ring stain of early years
    Effaced by every drop that steals.
The fruitless showers of worldly woe
    Fall dark to earth, and never rise;
While tears that from repentance flow,
    In bright exhalement reach the skies.
        Go, let me weep!

Leave me to sigh o'er hours that flew
    More idly than the summer's wind,
And, while they pass'd, a fragrance threw
    But left no trace of sweets behind.
The warmest sigh that pleasure heaves
    Is cold, is faint to those that swell
The heart, where pure repentance grieves
    O'er hours of pleasure loved too well!
        Leave me to sigh.

COME NOT, O LORD!

COME not, O Lord! in the dread robe of splendor
    Thou wor'st on the Mount, in the day of thine ire;
Come veiled in those shadows, deep, awful, but tender,
    Which mercy flings over thy features of fire!

Lord! thou remember'st the night, when thy nation*
   Stood fronting her foe by the red-rolling stream;
O'er Egypt thy pillar shed dark desolation,
   While Israel bask'd all the night in its beam.

So, when the dread clouds of anger enfold Thee
   From us, in thy mercy, the dark side remove;
While shrouded in terrors the guilty behold Thee,
   O turn upon us the mild light of thy Love!

WERE NOT THE SINFUL MARY'S TEARS.

WERE not the sinful Mary's tears
   An offering worthy Heaven,
When, o'er the faults of former years,
   She wept — and was forgiven? —

When bringing every balmy sweet
   Her day of luxury stored,
She o'er her Saviour's hallow'd feet
   The precious odors poured; —

And wiped them with that golden hair,
   Where once the diamond shone,
Though now those gems of grief were there
   Which shine for God alone!

---

* " And it came between the camp of the Egyptians and the camp of Israel: and it was a cloud and darkness to them, but it gave light by night to these." Exod. xiv. 20. My application of this passage is borrowed from some late prose writer, whose name I am ungrateful enough to forget.

Were not those sweets so humbly shed, —
  That hair — those weeping eyes, —
And the sunk heart, that inly bled, —
  Heaven's noblest sacrifice?

Thou that hast slept in error's sleep,
  O wouldst thou wake in heaven,
Like Mary kneel, like Mary weep,
  "Love much,"* — and be forgiven!

AS DOWN IN THE SUNLESS RETREATS.

AS down in the sunless retreats of the ocean,
  Sweet flowers are springing no mortal can see,
So, deep in my soul the still prayer of devotion,
  Unheard by the world, rises silent to thee,
    My God! silent to thee —
    Pure, warm, silent, to thee.

As still to the star of its worship, though clouded,
  The needle points faithfully o'er the dim sea,
So, dark as I roam, in this wintry world shrouded,
  The hope of my spirit turns trembling to thee,
    My God! trembling to thee —
    True, fond, trembling, to thee.

---

* "Her sins, which are many, are forgiven; for she loved much."—ST. LUKE vii. 47.

BUT WHO SHALL SEE.

BUT who shall see the glorious day,
    When, throned on Zion's brow,
The Lord shall rend that veil away
    Which hides the nations now !*
When earth no more beneath the fear
    Of his rebuke shall lie ;†
When pain shall cease, and every tear
    Be wiped from every eye !‡

Then, Judah ! thou no more shalt mourn
    Beneath the heathen's chain ;
Thy days of splendor shall return,
    And all be new again.§
The Fount of Life shall then be quaffed
    In peace by all who come ! ||
And every wind that blows shall waft
    Some long-lost exile home !

---

* " And he will destroy in this mountain the face of the covering cast over all people, and the veil that is spread over all nations."—Isa. xxv. 7.

† " The rebuke of his people shall he take away from off all the earth."—Isa. xxv. 8.

‡ " And God shall wipe away all tears from their eyes ; neither shall there be any more pain."—Rev. xxi. 4.

§ " And he that sat upon the throne said, Behold I make all things new."—Rev. xxi. 5.

|| " And whosoever will, let him take the water of life freely."—Rev. xxii. 17.

SACRED SONGS.

ALMIGHTY GOD.

CHORUS OF PRIESTS.

ALMIGHTY God! when round thy shrine
The Palm-tree's heavenly branch we twine,*
(Emblem of Life's eternal ray,
And Love that " fadeth not away,")
We bless the flowers, expanded all,†
We bless the leaves that never fall,
And trembling say, " In Eden thus
The Tree of Life may flower for us!"

When round thy Cherubs — smiling calm
Without their flames §—we wreath the palm,
O God! we feel the emblem true, —
Thy mercy is eternal too!
Those Cherubs with their smiling eyes,
That crown of palm which never dies,
Are but the types of Thee above —
Eternal Life, and Peace, and Love.

* " Scriptures having declared that the Temple of Jerusalem was a type of the Messiah, it is natural to conclude that the PALMS, which made so conspicuous a figure in that structure, represented that LIFE and IMMORTALITY which were brought to light by the Gospel."—Observations on the Palm, as a sacred Emblem, by W. Tigh.

† " And he carved all the walls of the house round about with carved figures of cherubims, and palm-trees, and OPEN FLOWERS." —1 KINGS vi. 29.

§ " When the passover of the tabernacles was revealed to the great law-giver in the mount, then the cherubic images which appeared in that structure were no longer surrounded by flames: for the tabernacle was a type of the dispensation of mercy, by which Jehovah confirmed his gracious covenant to redeem mankind."— Observations on the Palm.

O FAIR! O PUREST!

SAINT AUGUSTINE TO HIS SISTER.*

O FAIR! O purest! be thou the dove
   That flies alone to some sunny grove,
And lives unseen, and bathes her wing,
All vestal white, in the limpid spring.
There, if the hovering hawk be near,
That limpid spring in its mirror clear
Reflects him, ere he can reach his prey,
And warns the timorous bird away.
      Be thou this dove;
Fairest! purest! be thou this dove.

The sacred pages of God's own book
Shall be the spring, the eternal brook,
In whose holy mirror, night and day,
Thou'lt study Heaven's reflected ray :—
And should the foes of virtue dare,
With gloomy wing, to seek thee there,
Thou wilt see how dark their shadows lie
Between Heaven and thee, and trembling fly!
      Be thou that dove;
Fairest! purest! be thou that dove.

---

* In St. Augustine's treatise upon the advantages of a solitary life, addressed to his sister, there is the following fanciful passage, from which the thought of this song is taken: ' Te, soror, nunquam nolo esse securam, sed timere, semperque tuam fragilitatem habere suspectam, ad instar pavidæ columbæ frequentare rivos aquarum et quasi in speculo accipitris cernere supervolantis effigiem et cavere. Rivi aquarum sententiæ sunt scripturarum, quæ de limpidissimo sapientia fonte profluentes," etc. etc.— DE VIT. EREMIT. AD SOROREM.

ANGEL OF CHARITY.

ANGEL of Charity, who, from above
   Comes to dwell a pilgrim here,
Thy voice is music, thy smile is love,
   And pity's soul is in thy tear!
When on the shrine of God were laid
   First-fruits of all most good and fair,
That ever bloom'd in Eden's shade,
   Thine was the holiest offering there!

Hope and her sister, Faith, were given
   But as our guides to yonder sky;
Soon as they reach the verge of heaven,
   There, lost in perfect bliss, they die.*
But long as Love, almighty Love,
   Shall on his throne of thrones abide,
Thou, Charity, shalt dwell above,
   Smiling forever by His side.

BEHOLD THE SUN.

BEHOLD the Sun, how bright
   From yonder east he springs,
As if the soul of life and light
   Were breathing from his wings.

---

* " Then Faith shall fail, and holy Hope shall die,
  One lost in certainty, and one in joy."   PRIOR.

So bright the Gospel broke
  Upon the souls of men;
So fresh the dreaming world awoke
  In truth's full radiance then!

Before yon Sun arose,
  Stars clustered through the sky —
But O, how dim, how pale were those,
  To his one burning eye!

So Truth lent many a ray,
  To bless the Pagan's night —
But, Lord, how weak, how cold were they
  To Thy one glorious light!

LORD, WHO SHALL BEAR THAT DAY.

LORD, who shall bear that day, so dread, so splendid,
  When we shall see thy angel hovering o'er
This sinful world, with hand to heaven extended,
  And hear him swear by Thee that time's no more?*
When earth shall feel thy fast-consuming ray—
Who, mighty God! O who shall bear that day?

* And the Angel which I saw stand upon the sea and upon the earth lifted up his hand to heaven, and sware by Him that liveth for ever and ever, that there should be time no longer." REV. x. 5.

When thro' the world thy awful call hath sounded,
  "Wake, all ye dead, to judgment wake, ye dead!"†
And from the clouds, by seraph eyes surrounded,
  The Savior shall put forth his radiant head;‡
While earth and heaven before him pass away—||
Who, mighty God! O who shall bear that day?

When, with a glance, the eternal Judge shall sever
  Earth's evil spirits from the pure and bright,
And say to those, 'Depart from me forever!'
  To these, 'Come dwell with me in endless light!'§
When each and all in silence take their way —
Who, mighty God! O who shall bear that day?

O TEACH ME TO LOVE THEE.

O TEACH me to love thee, to feel what thou art,
  Till, filled with the one sacred image, my heart
    Shall all other passions disown —
Like some pure temple that shines apart,
    Reserved for thy worship alone!

---

† "Awake, ye dead, and come to judgment."

‡ They shall see the son of man coming in the clouds of heaven, and all the angels with him.—MAT. xxiv. 30.

|| From whose face the earth and the heaven fled away. REV. xx.

§ And before Him shall be gathered all nations, and He shall separate them one from another. Then shall the King say unto them on his right hand, Come, ye blessed of my Father, inherit the kingdom prepared for you, &c. Then shall he say also unto them on the left hand, Depart from me, ye cursed, &c. And these shall go away into everlasting punishment; but the righteous into life eternal.—MAT. xxv. 32.

In joy and in sorrow, thro' praise and thro' blame,
Thus still let me, living and dying the same,
    In *Thy* service bloom and decay —
Like some lone altar, whose votive flame
    In holiness wasteth away!

Tho' born in this desert, and doomed by my birth
To pain and affliction, to darkness and dearth,
    On Thee let my spirit rely —
Like some rude dial, that, fixed on earth,
    Still looks for its light from the sky!

WEEP, CHILDREN OF ISRAEL.

WEEP, weep for him, the Man of God —*
    In yonder vale he sunk to rest;
But none of earth can point the sod†
    That flowers above his sacred breast.
    Weep, children of Israel, weep!

His doctrine fell like Heaven's rain,‡
    His words refreshed like Heaven's dew —
O, ne'er shall Israel see again
    A Chief, to God and her so true.
    Weep, children of Israel, weep!

* And the children of Israel wept for Moses in the plains of Moab. DEUT. xxxiv: 8.

† And he buried him in a valley in the land of Moab: but no man knoweth of his sepulchre unto this day. DEUT. xxxiv: 6.

‡ My doctrine shall drop as the rain, my speech shall distil as the dew. MOSES' SONG, DEUT. xxxii: 2.

SACRED SONGS.

Remember ye his parting gaze,
  His farewell song by Jordan's tide,
When, full of glory and of days,
  He saw the promised land—and died! *
    Weep, children of Israel, weep!

Yet died he not as men who sink,
  Before our eyes, to soulless clay;
But, changed to spirit, like a wink
  Of summer lightning, passed away! †
    Weep, children of Israel, weep!

LIKE MORNING.

LIKE morning, when her early breeze
  Breaks up the surface of the seas
That, in those furrows, dark with night,
Her hand may sow the seeds of light—

Thy grace can send its breathings o'er
The spirit, dark and lost before,
And, freshening all its depths, prepare
For truth divine to enter there!

---

* I have caused thee to see it with thine eyes, but thou shalt not go over thither. DEUT. xxxii: 4.

† As he was going to embrace Eleazer and Joshua, and was still discoursing with them, a cloud stood over him on the sudden, and he disappeared in a certain valley, although he wrote in the Holy Books, that he died, which was done out of fear, lest they should venture to say that, because of his extraordinary virtue, he went to God. JOSEPHUS, BOOK IV. CHAP. 8.

Till David touched his sacred lyre,
In silence lay th' unbreathing wire ;
But, when he swept its chords along,
Even angels stooped to hear that song.

So sleeps the soul, till Thou, O Lord,
Shalt deign to touch its lifeless chord —
Till, waked by Thee, its breath shall rise
In music, worthy of the skies !

COME, YE DISCONSOLATE.

COME, ye disconsolate, where'er you languish,
    Come, at God's altar fervently kneel ;
Here bring your wounded hearts, here tell your anguish —
    Earth has no sorrow that Heaven cannot heal.

Joy of the desolate, Light of the straying,
    Hope, when all others die, fadeless and pure,
Here speaks the Comforter, in God's name saying—
    " Earth has no sorrow that Heaven cannot cure."

Go, ask the infidel, what boon he brings us,
    What charm for aching hearts *he* can reveal,
Sweet as that heavenly promise Hope sings us—
    " Earth has no sorrow that God cannot heal."

AWAKE, ARISE.

AWAKE, arise, thy light is come ;*
   The nations, that before outshone thee,
Now at thy feet lie dark and dumb —
   The glory of the Lord is on thee !

Arise—the Gentiles to thy ray,
   From every nook of earth shall cluster ;
And kings and princes haste to pay
   Their homage to thy rising lustre.§

Lift up thine eyes around, and see,
   O'er foreign fields, o'er farthest waters,
Thy exiled sons return to thee,
   To thee return thy home-sick daughters. †

And camels rich, from Midian's tents,
   Shall lay their treasures down before thee ;
And Saba bring her gold and scents,
   To fill thine air, and sparkle o'er thee.‡

---

* Arise, shine ; for thy light is come, and the glory of the Lord is risen upon thee. ISAIAH lx.

§ And the gentiles shall come to thy light, and kings to the brightness of thy rising. ISAIAH lx.

† Lift up thine eyes round about and see ; all they gather themselves together, they come to thee : thy sons shall come from afar and thy daughters shall be nursed at thy side. ISAIAH lx.

‡ The multitude of Camels shall cover thee ; the dromedaries of Midian and Ephah ; all they from Sheba shall come ; they shall bring gold and incense. ISAIAH lx.

See who are these that, like a cloud,*
    Are gathering from all earth's dominions,
Like doves, long absent, when allowed
    Homeward to shoot their trembling pinions.

Surely the isles shall wait for me, †
    The ships of Tarshish round will hover,
To bring thy sons across the sea,
    And waft their gold and silver over.

And, Lebanon, thy pomp shall grace — ‡
    The fir, the pine, the palm victorious
Shall beautify our Holy Place,
    And make the ground I tread on glorious.

No more shall discord haunt thy ways,§
    Nor ruin waste thy cheerless nation;
But thou shalt call thy portals, Praise,
    And thou shalt name thy walls, Salvation.

---

* Who are these that fly as a cloud, and as the doves to their windows. ISAIAH lx.

† Surely the isles shall wait for me, and the ships of Tarshish first, to bring thy sons from far, their silver and their gold with them. ISAIAH lx.

‡ The glory of Lebanon shall come unto thee; the fir-tree, the pine-tree, and the box together, to beautify the place of my sanctuary, and I will make the place of my feet glorious. ISAIAH lx.

§ Violence shall no more be heard in thy land, wasting nor destruction within thy borders; but thou shalt call thy walls Salvation, and thy gates Praise. ISAIAH lx.

The sun no more shall make thee bright,†
  Nor moon shall lend her lustre to thee;
But God himself shall be thy light,
  And flash eternal glory through thee.

Thy sun shall never more go down;
  A ray, from Heaven itself descended,
Shall light thy everlasting crown —
  Thy days of mourning all are ended.‡

My own, elect, and righteous Land!
  The Branch, forever green and vernal,
Which I have planted with this hand —
  Live thou shalt in Life Eternal.*

---

† Thy sun shall be no more thy light by day; neither for brightness shall the moon give light unto thee; but the Lord shall be unto thee an everlasting light, and thy God thy glory. ISAIAH lx.

‡ Thy sun shall no more go down, for the Lord shall be thine everlasting light, and the days of thy mourning shall be ended. ISAIAH lx.

* Thy people also shall be all righteous; they shall inherit the land forever, the branch of my planting, the work of my hands. ISAIAH lx.

THERE IS A BLEAK DESERT.

THERE is a bleak Desert, where daylight grows weary
Of wasting its smile on a region so dreary —
    What may that Desert be?
'T is Life, cheerless Life, where the few joys that come
Are lost, like that daylight, for 't is not their home.

There is a lone Pilgrim, before whose faint eyes
The water he pants for but sparkles and flies—
    Who may that Pilgrim be?
'T is Man, hapless Man, through his life tempted on
By fair shining hopes, that in shining are gone.

There is a bright Fountain, thro' that desert stealing,
To pure lips alone its refreshment revealing —
    What may that Fountain be?
'T is Truth, holy Truth, that, like springs under ground,
By the gifted of Heaven alone can be found.*

There is a fair Spirit, whose wand hath the spell
To point where those waters in secrecy dwell —
    Who may that Spirit be?
Tis Faith, humble Faith, who hath learnt that where'er
Her wand bends to worship, the Truth must be there.

---

* In singing, the following line had better be adopted:
  Can but by the gifted of Heaven be found.

SINCE FIRST THY WORD.

SINCE first thy word awaked my heart,
  Like new life dawning o'er me,
Where'er I turn mine eyes, Thou art,
  All light and love before me.
Nought else I feel, or hear, or see —
  All bonds of earth I sever —
Thee, O God, and only Thee
  I live for, now and ever.

Like him, whose fetters dropped away
  When light shone o'er his prison,*
My spirit, touched by Mercy's ray,
  Hath from her chains arisen.
And shall a soul Thou bid'st be free
  Return to bondage ? — never !
Thee, O God, and only Thee,
  I live for, now and ever.

---

* And, behold, the angel of the Lord came upon him, and a light shined in the prison, and his chains fell off from his hands. ACTS xii : 7.

HARK, 'TIS THE BREEZE.

HARK !—'t is the breeze of twilight calling
   Earth's weary children to repose ;
While round the couch of Nature falling,
   Gently the night's soft curtains close.

Soon o'er a world, in sleep reclining,
   Numberless stars, through yonder dark,
Shall look, like eyes of cherubs shining
   From out the veils that hid the Ark.

Guard us, O Thou, who never sleepest,
   Thou who, in silence throned above,
Throughout all time, unwearied, keepest
   Thy watch of Glory, Power, and Love.

Grant that, beneath thine eye, securely
   Our souls, awhile from life withdrawn,
May, in their darkness, stilly, purely,
   Like " sealed fountains," rest till dawn.

WHERE IS YOUR DWELLING, YE SAINTED?

WHERE is your dwelling, ye sainted?
    Through what Elysium more bright
Than fancy or hope ever painted,
    Walk ye in glory and light?
Who the same kingdom inherits?
    Breathes there a soul that may dare
Look to that world of Spirits?
    Or hope to dwell with you there?

Sages! who, even in exploring
    Nature through all her bright ways,
Went, like the seraphs, adoring,
    And veiled your eyes in the blaze —
Martyrs! who left for our reaping
    Truths you had sown in your blood —
Sinners! whom long years of weeping
    Chastened from evil to good —

Maidens! who, like the young Crescent,
    Turning away your pale brows
From earth, and the light of the Present,
    Looked to your Heavenly Spouse —
Say, through what region enchanted
    Walk ye, in heaven's sweet air?
Say, to what spirits 'tis granted,
    Bright souls, to dwell with you there?

Make bright the arrows, and gather the shields,§
    Set the standard of God on high —
Swarm we, like locusts, o'er all her fields,
    'Zion' our watchword, and 'Vengeance' our cry!
Woe! woe!—the time of thy visitation*
    Is come, proud Land, thy doom is cast —
And the black surge of desolation
    Sweeps o'er thy guilty head, at last!
        War, war, war, against Babylon!

---

§ Make bright the arrows; gather the shields . . . . set up the standard upon the walls of Babylon. JEREMIAH li.

* Woe unto them! for their day is come, the time of their visitation. JEREMIAH li.

INDEX.

IRISH MELODIES.

After the Battle	33
Alone in crowds to wander on	130
And doth not a meeting like this make amends	115
As a beam o'er the face of the waters may glow	11
As slow our ship her foamy track	83
As vanquish'd Erin wept beside	113
At the mid hour of night, when stars are weeping	55
Avenging and bright fall the swift sword of Erin	49
Before the Battle	32
Believe me, if all those endearing young charms	25
By that Lake whose gloomy shore	46
By the Feal's wave benighted	119
By the hope within us springing	32
Come o'er the sea	68
Come, rest in this bosom, my own stricken deer	76
Come, send round the wine, and leave points of belief	23
Dear Harp of my country! in darkness I found thee	81
Desmond's Song	119
Down in the valley come meet me to-night	100
Drink of this cup—you'll find there's a spell in	99
Drink to her who long	27
Echo	104
Erin! oh Erin!	26
Erin! the tear and the smile in thine eyes	4
Eveleen's Bower	19

INDEX TO THE MELODIES.

Fairest! put on awhile 112
Farewell!—but whenever you welcome the hour 64
Fill the bumper fair 79
Fly not yet; 'tis just the hour.......................... 7
Forget not the field where they perished 92
From this hour the pledge is given 140

Go where Glory waits thee 1

Has sorrow thy young days shaded...................... 69
Here we dwell, in holiest bowers 51
How dear to me the hour when daylight dies 14
How oft has the Benshee cried.......................... 16
How sweet the answer Echo makes 104

I'd mourn the hopes that leave me 67
If thou'lt be mine, the treasures of air 90
Ill Omens 31
In the morning of life, when its cares are unknown 84
In yonder valley there dwelt, alone.................... 117
I saw from the beach, when the morning was shining 78
I saw thy form in youthful prime 45
It is not the tear at this moment shed 38
I've a secret to tell thee, but hush! not here........... 131
I wish I was by that dim Lake......................... 121

Lay his sword by his side............................. 136
Lesbia hath a beaming eye............................. 43
Let Erin remember the days of old..................... 20
Like the bright lamp that shone in Kildare's holy fane 26
Love and the Novice 51
Love's young Dream 39

My gentle Harp, once more I waken 82

Nay, tell me not, dear, that the goblet drowns 48
Ne'er ask the hour—what is it to us 95
Night clos'd around the conqueror's way 33
No, not more welcome the fairy numbers 70

INDEX TO THE MELODIES.

O'Donohue's Mistress 102
Of all the fair months that round the sun 102
Oh Arranmore, lov'd Arranmore 135
Oh banquet not in those shining bowers 104
Oh blame not the bard, if he fly to the bowers 28
Oh breathe not his name, let it sleep in the shade 5
Oh could we do with this world of ours 137
Oh doubt me not 65
Oh for the swords of former time 94
Oh had we some bright little isle of our own 63
Oh haste and leave this sacred isle 12
Oh the days are gone, when Beauty bright 39
Oh the sight entrancing 108
Oh the Shamrock 53
Oh think not my spirits are always as light 8
Oh 'tis sweet to think that where'er we rove 61
Oh weep for the hour 19
Oh where's the slave so lowly 75
Oh, ye Dead! oh, ye Dead! whom we know 101
On Music 37
One bumper at parting, tho' many 56

Quick! we have but a second 114

Remember the glories of Brien the Brave 3
Remember thee? yes, while there's life in this heart 86
Rich and rare were the gems she wore 10

Sail on, sail on, thou fearless bark 96
Shall the Harp then be silent, when he who first gave ... 106
She is far from the land where her young hero sleeps 47
She sung of Love, while o'er her lyre 123
Silent, oh Moyle, be the roar of thy water 22
Silence is in our festal halls 141
Sing—sing—Music was given 124
Sing, sweet Harp, oh sing to me 126
Song of Innisfail 132
Song of the Battle Eve 127
Strike the gay harp! see the moon is on high 133
St. Senanus and the Lady 12

INDEX TO MELODIES.

Sublime was the warning that Liberty spoke	23
Sweet Innisfallen, fare thee well	110
Take back the virgin page	14
The dawning of morn, the daylight's sinking	105
The dream of those days	139
Thee, thee, only thee	105
The Fortune-teller	100
The harp that once through Tara's halls	6
The Irish Peasant to his Mistress	35
The Legacy	15
The Meeting of the Waters	11
The Minstrel boy to the war is gone	60
The Mountain Sprite	117
The Night Dance	133
The Origin of the Harp	38
The Prince's Day	41
The Parallel	97
The Song of Fionnuala	22
The Song of O'Ruark	61
The time I've lost in wooing	74
The valley lay smiling before me	61
The Wandering Bard	129
The wine-cup is circling in Almhin's hall	138
The young May moon is beaming, love	59
There is not in the wide world a valley so sweet	11
There are sounds of mirth	134
They came from a land beyond the sea	132
They know not my heart, who believe there can be	121
They may rail at this life—from the hour I began it	93
This life is all chequered with pleasures and woes	52
Tho' dark are our sorrows, to-day we'll forget them	41
Though humble the banquet	125
Tho' the last glimpse of Erin with sorrow I see	9
Through Erin's Isle	53
Through grief and through danger	35
'Tis believ'd that this Harp	33
'Tis gone, and for ever, the light we saw breaking	77
'Tis sweet to think, that, where'er we rove	34
'Tis the last rose of summer	58

INDEX TO MELODIES.

To Ladies' eyes around, boy	91
To-morrow, comrade, we	127
'Twas one of those dreams that by music are brought	111
War Song	3
Weep on, weep on, your hour is past	42
We may roam thro' this world, like a child at a feast	18
What life like that of the bard can be	129
What the bee is to the floweret	51
When cold in the earth lies the friend thou hast lov'd	85
When daylight was yet sleeping under the billow	31
Whene'er I see those smiling eyes	89
When first I met thee, warm and young	71
When he, who adores thee, has left but the name	5
When in death I shall calm recline	15
When thro' life unblest we rove	37
While gazing on the moon's light	30
While History's Muse the memorial was keeping	73
Wreath the bowl	87
Yes, sad one of Sion—if closely resembling	97
You remember Ellen, our hamlet's pride	66

SACRED SONGS.

Almighty God! when round thy shrine	159
Angel of Charity, who, from above	161
As down in the sunless retreats of the ocean	157
Awake, arise, thy light is come	167
Behold the sun, how bright	161
But who shall see the glorious day	158
Come not, O Lord! in the dread robe of splendor	155
Come, ye disconsolate, where'er you languish	166
Fallen is thy throne, O Israel	146
Go forth to the Mount—bring the olive-branch home	175
Go, let me weep, there's bliss in tears	155

INDEX TO SACRED SONGS.

Hark!—'tis the breeze of twilight calling 172
How lightly mounts the Muse's wing 174

Is it not sweet to think, hereafter 176

Like morning, when her early breeze 165
Lord who shall bear that day, so dread, so splendid 162

O fair! O purest! be thou the dove 160
O Thou who dry'st the mourner's tear 150
O teach me to love thee, to feel what thou art 163

Since first thy word awaked my heart 171
Sound the loud timbrel o'er Egypt's dark sea 154

The bird, let loose in eastern skies 149
There is a bleak Desert, where daylight grows weary 170
The turf shall be my fragrant shrine 152
This world is all a fleeting show 147
Thou art, O God! the life and light 145

War against Babylon shout we around 177
Weep not for those whom the veil of the tomb 151
Weep, weep for him, the Man of God 164
Were not the sinful Mary's tears 156
Where is your dwelling, ye sainted 173
Who is the maid my spirit seeks 148